SOUNDS OF LANGUAGE

readers

SOUNDS
OF MYSTERY
BY BILL MARTIN, JR.

 Holt, Rinehart and Winston, Inc., New York, Toronto, London

Acknowledgments

The Author and Holt, Rinehart and Winston, Inc., thank the following authors, publishers, agents and parties whose help and permissions to reprint materials have made this book possible. If any errors in acknowledgments have occurred, the errors were inadvertent and will be corrected in subsequent editions as they are realized.

Abelard-Schuman Ltd., New York, for "Pussy-Willows," reprinted from *Runny Days, Sunny Days,* by Aileen Fisher, by permission of Abelhard-Schuman Ltd. All rights reserved. Copyright © 1958 by Aileen Fisher.

Appleton-Century-Crofts, Inc., for "The Flower-Fed Buffaloes," from *Going to the Stars,* by Vachel Lindsay. © 1926 by D. Appleton and Company; © 1954 by Appleton-Century-Crofts, Inc.

Aaron Ashley, Inc., New York, for the painting "The Smoke Signal," on pages 50-51.

Atheneum House, Inc., for "Alligator on the Escalator," from *Catch a Little Rhyme.* Copyright © 1966 by Eve Merriam. Used by permission of Atheneum Publishers.

Burke and Van Heusen, Inc., for "Swinging on a Star" by Johnny Burke. © 1944 by Burke and Van Heusen, Inc.

Central Soya, for the illustration "Operation Moonbean" on page 207. Courtesy of Central Soya.

Creole Petroleum Corporation, for their kind permission to use the painting of a Maracaibo beach, on pages 182–183, by Lourdes Armas de Antillano, which appeared in their company publication, *El Farol.*

Curtis Brown Ltd., New York, for "The Hunter" by Ogden Nash, from *Versus,* by Ogden Nash. Copyright © 1947 by Ogden Nash. Reprinted by permission of Curtis Brown Ltd.

Curtis Brown Ltd., New York, for "Jonathan Bing," from *Jonathan Bing and Other Poems,* by Beatrice Curtis Brown. Reprinted by permission of Curtis Brown Ltd. Copyright 1936 by Beatrice Curtis Brown; copyright renewed 1964.

Curtis Brown Ltd., New York, for "J's the Jumping Jay-Walker." Copyright © 1948 by Phyllis McGinley. Reprinted by permission.

Curtis Brown Ltd., New York, for "The Sniffle" by Ogden Nash, from *Verses from 1929 On,* by Ogden Nash. Copyright © 1941 by Ogden Nash. Reprinted by permission of Curtis Brown Ltd.

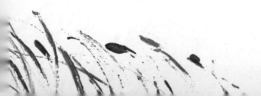

Harcourt, Brace & World, Inc., for the poem on page 101, "Why Did the Children Put Beans in Their Ears," from *The People, Yes,* by Carl Sandburg. Copyright 1936 by Harcourt, Brace & World, Inc.; copyright 1964 by Carl Sandburg. Reprinted by permission of the publishers.

Harper & Row, Publishers, for "Afternoon on a Hill" by Edna St. Vincent Millay, from *Collected Poems.* By permission of Norma Millay Ellis. Copyright 1917, 1945 by Edna St. Vincent Millay.

Harper & Row, Publishers, for "Escape," from *Charlotte's Web,* by E. B. White, pictures by Garth Williams. Copyright 1952 by E. B. White.

Harper & Row, Publishers, for "Full of the Moon," from the book, *In the Middle of the Trees,* by Karla Kuskin. Copyright © 1958 by Karla Kuskin.

Verlag Herder K. G., Freiburg, for illustrations from "Mool," from *Mool, der Maulwurf,* published by Verlag Herder K. G., Freiburg. Copyright by Verlag Herder K. G., Freiburg in Breisgau, Germany, 1962. English version herein copyright by Holt, Rinehart and Winston, Inc., 1967. Printed in U.S.A. All English rights reserved.

Mrs. Helen B. Herford, for "I Heard a Bird Sing" by Oliver B. Herford.

Holt, Rinehart and Winston, Inc., for "Bees," from *Buzz, Buzz, Buzzing Bees,* A Kin/Der Owl Book, by Gene Fulks, with pictures by Zena Bernstein. Copyright © 1967 by Holt, Rinehart and Winston, Inc. All rights reserved. Reprinted by permission of the publishers.

Holt, Rinehart & Winston, Inc., for Henry W. Ford's *Dr. Frick and His Fractions,* A Wise Owl Book. Copyright © 1965 by Holt, Rinehart and Winston, Inc.

Holt, Rinehart and Winston, Inc., for the illustrations of "History of the Ice Cream Cone," from *If You Can Count to 10,* A Young Owl Book, by Howard F. Fehr, with pictures by Eric Carle. Copyright © 1964 by Holt, Rinehart and Winston, Inc.

Holt, Rinehart and Winston, Inc., for *How Birds Keep Warm in Winter,* A Young Owl Book, written and illustrated by Bernard Martin. Copyright © 1964 by Holt, Rinehart and Winston, Inc. Reprinted by permission of the publishers.

Holt, Rinehart and Winston, Inc., for "The Last Word of a Bluebird," from *Complete Poems of Robert Frost.* Copyright 1916, 1923 by Holt, Rinehart and Winston, Inc.; copyright 1944, 1951, by Robert Frost. Reprinted by permission of Holt, Rinehart and Winston, Inc.

Holt, Rinehart and Winston, Inc., for "October," from *Complete Poems of Robert Frost.* Copyright 1934 by Holt, Rinehart and Winston, Inc.; copyright © 1962 by Robert Frost. Reprinted by permission.

Holt, Rinehart and Winston, Inc., for "The Pasture," from *You Come Too,* by Robert Frost. Copyright © 1939; © 1967 by Holt, Rinehart and Winston, Inc. Reprinted by permission of Holt, Rinehart and Winston, Inc.

Holt, Rinehart and Winston, Inc., for the illustration appearing on page 76 (A Schematic View of the Circulatory System), by Pauline Larivière, from *Modern Health,* by James H. Otto, Cloyd J. Julian, and J. Edward Tether. Copyright © 1967 by Holt, Rinehart and Winston, Inc.; previous editions copyright © 1955, 1959, 1963 by Holt, Rinehart and Winston, Inc. All rights reserved. Reprinted by permission of the publisher.

Holt, Rinehart and Winston, Inc., for "Someone," from *Collected Poems 1901–1918,* by Walter de la Mare. Copyright 1920 by Henry Holt and Company; copyright 1948 by Walter de la Mare.

Honeywell, Inc., for their kind permission to use the pictures accompanying the essay "Plugging into Meanings." Courtesy of Honeywell Electronic Data Processing.

Estelle Mandel, Agent for Creative Artists, New York, for exceptional service in expediting art assignments for this book.

Helen Irish May, for permission to use her poem, "The Robin."

McGraw-Hill Book Company, for "The Day the Numbers Disappeared," from *The Day the Numbers Disappeared* by Leonard Simon. Copyright © 1963 by Leonard Simon and Jeanne Bendick, McGraw-Hill Book Company. Used by permission.

Natural History Magazine, The Journal of the American Museum of Natural History, New York, for the paintings by Basil Ede, accompanying the picture story herein, "Birds in a Gallery," from the December issue of *Natural History*.

Hugh Noyes, for the poem, "Daddy Fell into the Pond" by Alfred Noyes, on page 281. Used by permission.

Oxford University Press, Inc., London, Publishers, for "Giant Thunder," from the book, *The Blackbird in the Lilac*, by James Reeves.

Laurence Pollinger Ltd., Authors' Agents, London, for the selection "But Toads Don't Bite," from "The Pomegranate Tree" from the book, *My Name Is Aram*, by William Saroyan, published by Faber and Faber Ltd.

Laurence Pollinger Ltd., Authors' Agents, London, for "The Pasture," from *Complete Poems of Robert Frost*, published by Jonathan Cape Ltd. Proprietors: Holt, Rinehart and Winston, Inc.

Laurence Pollinger Ltd., Authors' Agents, London, for "The Last Word of a Bluebird," from *Complete Poems of Robert Frost*, published by Jonathan Cape Ltd. Proprietors: Holt, Rinehart and Winston, Inc.

Laurence Pollinger Ltd., Authors' Agents, London, for "October," from *Complete Poems of Robert Frost*, published by Jonathan Cape Ltd. Proprietors: Holt, Rinehart and Winston, Inc.

Rand McNally & Company, for "The Conjure Wives," from *Happy Holidays,* by Francis Wicke. Copyright © 1921.

Paul R. Reynolds, Inc., agent for the author, for "George," from the book, *George,* by Agnes Sligh Turnbull. Copyright © 1965 by Agnes Sligh Turnbull. Reprinted by permission of Paul R. Reynolds, Inc., 599 Fifth Ave., New York.

Charles Scribner's Sons, for "The Duel," from *Poems of Childhood*, by Eugene Field, published by Charles Scribner's Sons.

The Society of Authors, Representative for The Literary Trustees of Walter de la Mare, for "All but Blind," by Walter de la Mare.

The Society of Authors, Representative for The Literary Trustees of Walter de la Mare, for "Someone," by Walter de la Mare.

Wayfarer Music, Inc., New York, for "My Old 'Coon Dog," lyrics and music by Burl Ives. Copyright © 1961 by Wayfarer Music, Inc. Used by permission.

Williamson Music, Inc., New York, and Williamson Music Ltd., London, for "My Favorite Things," from *The Sound of Music*. Copyright © 1959 by Richard Rodgers and Oscar Hammerstein, II. Used by permission of the publisher.

TABLE OF CONTENTS
PART I
FIGURING OUT HOW READING WORKS

PART II

RESPONDING TO READING

SOMEONE

came knocking
  At my wee, small door;
Someone came knocking
  I'm *sure...sure...sure,*
I listened, I opened,
  I looked to left and right,
But *nought there was a-stirring*
  In the still, dark night;
Only the busy beetle
  Tap-tapping in the wall,
Only from the forest
  The screech owl's call,
Only the cricket whistling
  While the dewdrops fall,
So I know not who came knocking,
  At all...at all...at all.

A poem by
Walter de la Mare

Have you ever heard the wind go Yooooo?
'Tis a pitiful sound to hear!
It seems to chill you through and through
With a strange and speechless fear.
'Tis the voice of the night that broods outside
When folk should be asleep,
And many and many's the time I've cried
To the darkness brooding far and wide
Over the land and the deep:
"Whom do you want,
O lonely night,
That you wail the long hours through?"
And the night would say
In its ghostly way:

Yoooooooooooooo
Yoooooooooooooo
Yoooooooooooooo

My mother told me long ago (When I was a little tad)
That when the night went wailing so,
Somebody had been bad;
And then, when I was snug in bed,
Whither I had been sent,
With the blankets pulled up round my head,
I'd think of what my mother'd said,
And wonder what boy she meant!

The Night Wind

A poem by Eugene Field,
picture by George Buckett

The Shinny Bone

A story told by Dupris Knight about 1882

Once there was a woman who went out to pick beans,
and she found a Shinny Bone.
She took the Shinny Bone home with her,
and that night when she went to bed,
the wind began to moan and groan.
Away off in the distance
she seemed to hear a voice crying,

> "Who's got my Shin-n-n-ny Bo-o-o-n-e?
> Who's got my Shin-n-n-ny Bo-o-o-n-e?"

The wind rose and began to screech
around the house,
and the woman covered her head with the quilts.
The voice seemed to come nearer:

> "Who's got my Shin-n-n-ny Bo-o-o-n-e?"

The woman scrooched down,
'way down under the covers,
and 'bout that time
the wind 'peared to hit the house,

SWOOOOOOSH,

and the old house creaked and cracked
like somethin' was tryin' to get in.

The voice had come nearer, almost at the door now,

and it said,

"Where's my Shin-n-n-ny Bo-o-o-n-e?

Who's got my Shin-n-n-ny Bo-o-o-n-e?"

The woman scrooched further down under the covers
and pulled them tight around her head.
The wind growled around the house
like some big animal
and r-r-rumbled over the chimbley.
All at once she heard the door
cr-r-rack open,
and Somethin' slipped in
and began to creep over the floor.
The floor would cre-e-eak,
cre-e-eak at every step
that Thing took toward her bed.
The woman could almost feel it
bending over her head over the bed.
Then in an awful voice it said,
"Where's my Shin-n-n-n-ny Bo-o-o-o-n-e?
Who's got my Shin-n-n-n-ny Bo-o-o-o-n-e?"

"YOU GOT IT!!!"

Adapted by Bill Martin, Jr.,
from a German story *Mool,*
by Klaus Winter and
Helmut Bischoff.

Something in the earth
is digging upward,
digging upward,
moving and lifting,
lifting and pushing,
pressing outward,
pressing upward and downward.

Who is it that is digging, that seems to be stuck in the ground? It is Mool, the mole.

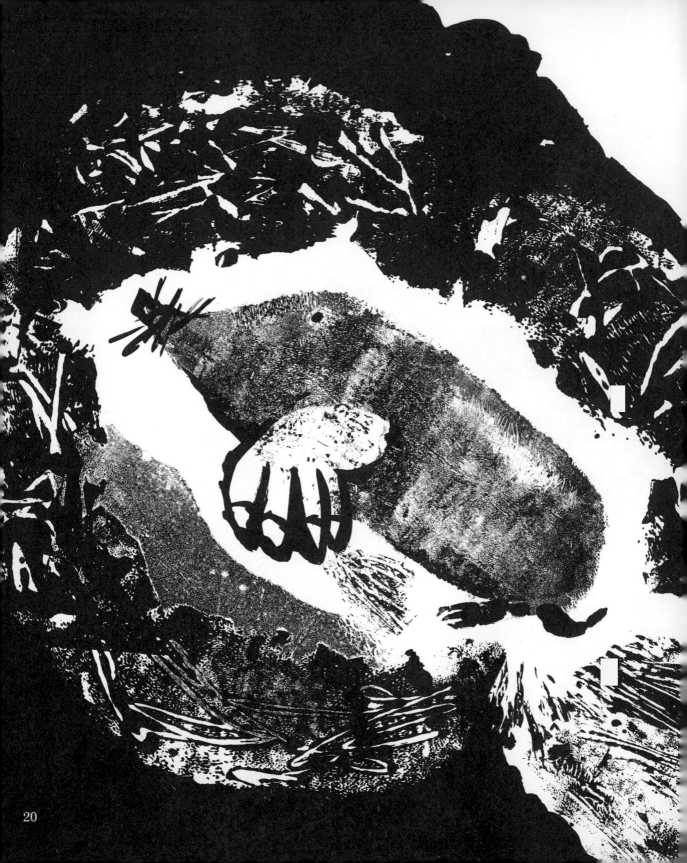

He is small and black,
with tiny eyes
that scarcely see
and two giant flippers
that are good for digging.
He has a snout and a long beard.
His body is covered
with velvety fur.
Mool, the mole,
crafty and shy,
constantly hungry.

the earth. He digs a tunnel to the sweet ivy roots.

He digs a hole to cool water.
He digs a pipeline
to the bed of young turnips.
Wherever he goes,
he digs a hole,
a tunnel, a pipeline.
Mool, the mole, is a digger.

But where does the earth go
when Mool is digging a hole?
Up, up, out of the hole.
He pushes the dirt
out of his tunnel.
Up with it! Out with it!
He leaves a mountain of dirt
at the mouth of his tunnel.
Mool is a pesky animal
if he digs in your yard.

Now Mool is playing.

He is playing with a centipede
caught in his passageways.
He is playing with a worm
and a cricket and a snail.
They, too, are caught in the tunnel.

Smack!

Crackle!

Slurp

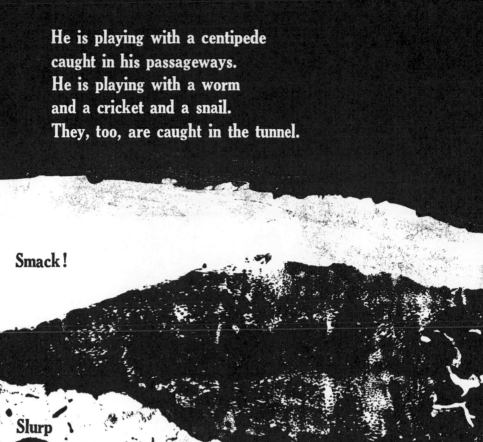

Mool has eaten them.
He has filled his stomach,
and now he is drowsy.
The mole is going to sleep.

From far at the end
of his passageways
come the sounds
of crawling and puffing,
puffing and scratching.
Mool hears it.
He's on his feet.
>   After them!
>   Out with them!
The fur tousles!
>   They squeal!
>   They squeak!
He chases the mouse sisters
out of his tunnel.

Mool wants to be alone.

Smack! Slap!
Mool is digging upward.
Suddenly, he is out of the ground.
Oh, how light it is!
The sun blinds him,
but it is warm on his fur.
He lies down to sleep
at the mouth of his tunnel.
High above him,
high in the clouds,
there is a black spot
that Mool does not see.

The spot has keen eyes
and sharp, pointed claws.
It dives from the sky
like a big shadow
. . . getting bigger
. . . bigger
. . . gigantic!
A fierce, hungry buzzard
is diving down at Mool!
Mool squeals!
He scuttles back into the ground.
The buzzard flies away
with only a stone in its claws.

Mool digs deeper and wider.
He is hungry again.
His stomach can bear
something tasty!
And what has he found?
A fat turnip.
    Crunch, crunch!
A beautiful cabbage.
    Crunch, crunch!
A garden filled
with tasty, fresh vegetables.
    Crunch, crunch!
And here comes the farmer,
the angry farmer.
Here he comes with a frown,
waving his shovel.

But Mool escapes.
He scuttles deep in his burrows.
No one can catch Mool
with a shovel.
"If I can't catch him,"
says the farmer,
"then I will drive him away.
I'll stick oily rags
in his burrows
to make a terrible smell.
And I'll put empty bottles
in his burrows
to whistle in the wind."

Mool stops.
"What do I smell?
What is that noise?
Oh, what a foul smell!
Oh, what a dreadful racket!
Away from here,
as fast as possible!
My delicate ears,
my sensitive nose
cannot bear this!"

Mool runs out of his burrow.
He swims across the lake,
his head above water.
On the other shore,
Mool starts burrowing
a new hole in the ground
with passageways all around
and a mountain of dirt
on the grass.

This
is the way
it is
with Mool,
mole
in the
ground.

All but blind
   In his chambered hole
Gropes for worms
   The four-clawed Mole.

All but blind
   In the evening sky,
The hooded Bat
   Twirls softly by.

All but blind
   In the burning day
The Barn-Owl blunders
   On the way.

And blind as are
   These three to me,
So, blind to Someone
   I must be.

ALL BUT BLIND

A poem by Walter de la Mare

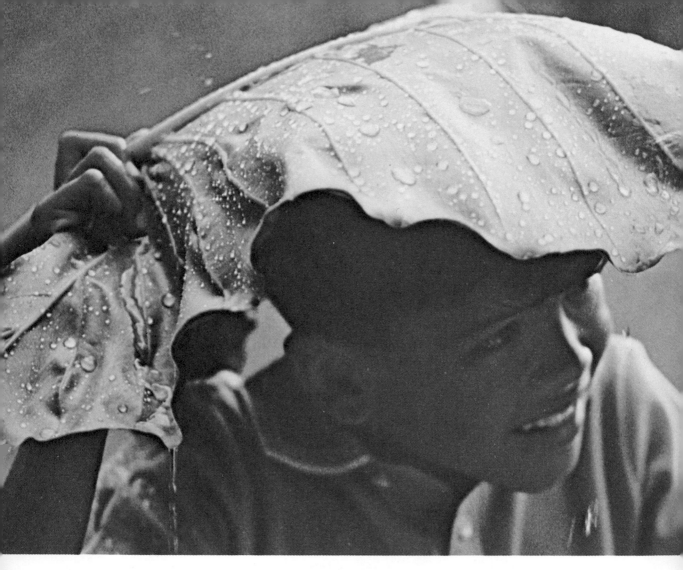

Spring Rain

The storm came up so very quick
    It couldn't have been quicker.
I should have brought my hat along,
    I should have brought my slicker.

My hair is wet, my feet are wet,
    I couldn't be much wetter.
I fell into a river once
    But this is even better.

A poem by Marchette Chute,
photograph by Dennis Stock

Rain Sizes

Rain comes in various sizes.
Some rain is as small as a mist.
It tickles your face with surprises,
And tingles as if you'd been kissed.

Some rain is the size of a sprinkle
And doesn't put out all the sun.
You can see the drops sparkle and twinkle,
And a rainbow comes out when it's done.

Some rain is as big as a nickel
And comes with a crash and a hiss.
It comes down too heavy to tickle.
It's more like a splash than a kiss.

When it rains the right size
    and you're wrapped in
Your rainclothes, it's fun out of doors.
But run home before you get trapped in
The big rain that rattles and roars.

A poem by John Ciardi

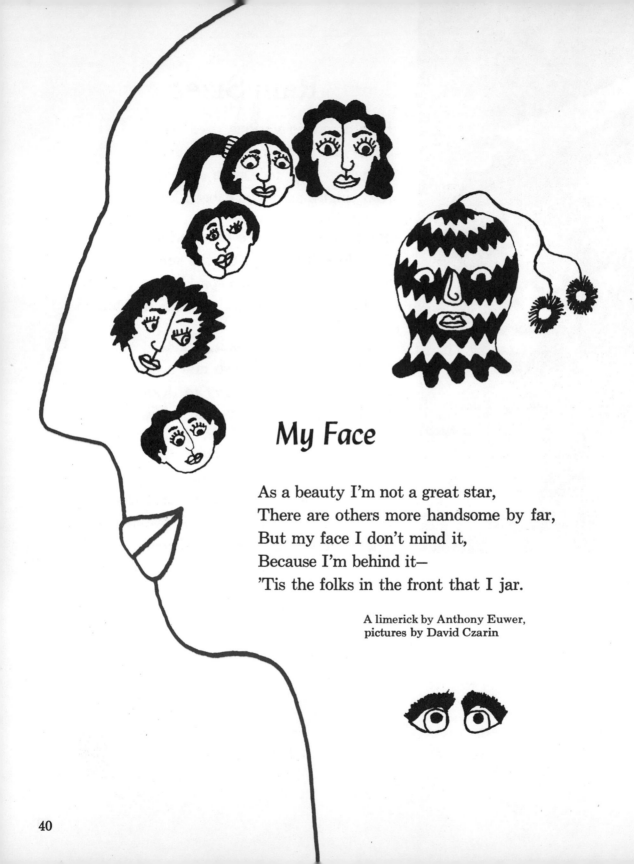

My Face

As a beauty I'm not a great star,
There are others more handsome by far,
But my face I don't mind it,
Because I'm behind it—
'Tis the folks in the front that I jar.

A limerick by Anthony Euwer,
pictures by David Czarin

Escape

This humorous episode from the novel Charlotte's Web *by E. B. White is a memorable picture of Wilbur, a friendly pig, and of the goose,
a rabble-rouser. Even if you have read the
book, this story will bring back pleasant memories of one of the great modern-time books for
boys and girls. If you have not read* Charlotte's
Web, *this story will invite you to get the complete story from the library or bookstore for
reading. The pictures by Garth Williams are
as much a part of the story as the words. They
are reprinted here from the original book.*

One afternoon in June,
when Wilbur was
almost two months old,
he wandered out
into his small yard
outside the barn.
Fern had not arrived
for her usual visit.
Wilbur stood in the sun
feeling lonely and bored.

"There's never anything to do
around here," he thought.
He walked slowly
to his food trough and sniffed
to see if anything
had been overlooked at lunch.
He found a small strip
of potato skin and ate it.
His back itched,
so he leaned against the fence
and rubbed against the boards.
When he tired of this,
he walked indoors,
climbed to the top
of the manure pile,
and sat down.
He didn't feel
like going to sleep,
he didn't feel like digging,
he was tired of standing still,
tired of lying down.

"I'm less than two months old
  and I'm tired of living," he said.
He walked out
  to the yard again.

"When I'm out here," he said,
"there's no place to go but in.
When I'm indoors,
  there's no place to go
  but out in the yard."

"That's where you're wrong,
  my friend," said a voice.

Wilbur looked
  through the fence
  and saw the goose
  standing there.

"You don't have to stay
  in that dirty-little, dirty-little,
  dirty-little yard,"
  said the goose,
  who talked rather fast.
"One of the boards is loose.
  Push on it,
  push-push-push on it,
  and come on out!"

"What?" said Wilbur.
"Say it slower!"

"At-at-at, at the risk
  of repeating myself,"
  said the goose,
"I suggest that you come on out.
  It's wonderful out here."

"Did you say
  a board was loose?"

"That I did, that I did,"
  said the goose.

Wilbur walked up to the fence
  and saw that the goose was right
—one board was loose.
He put his head down,
  shut his eyes, and pushed.
The board gave way.

Fern Zuckerman, who appears in the picture
above, is Wilbur's friend.

In a minute he had squeezed
through the fence
and was standing
in the long grass outside his yard.
The goose chuckled.

"How does it feel to be free?"
she asked.

"I like it," said Wilbur.
"That is, I *guess* I like it."
Actually, Wilbur felt queer
to be outside his fence,
with nothing between him
and the big world.

"Where do you think
I'd better go?"

"Anywhere you like,
anywhere you like,"
said the goose.
"Go down through the orchard,
root up the sod!
Go down through the garden,
dig up the radishes!
Root up everything!
Eat grass! Look for corn!
Look for oats!
Run all over!

Skip and dance,
jump and prance!
Go down through the orchard
and stroll in the woods!
The world is a wonderful place
when you're young."

"I can see that," replied Wilbur.
He gave a jump in the air,
twirled, ran a few steps,
stopped, looked all around,
sniffed the smells of afternoon,
and then set off walking
down through the orchard.
Pausing in the shade
of an apple tree,
he put his strong snout
into the ground
and began pushing,
digging, and rooting.
He felt very happy.
He had plowed up
quite a piece of ground
before anyone noticed him.

Mrs. Zuckerman was the first
to see him.
She saw him
from the kitchen window.

She immediately shouted
for the men.
"Homer! Pig's out!
Lurvy! Pig's out!
Homer! Lurvy! Pig's out.
He's down there
under that apple tree."

"Now the trouble starts."
thought Wilbur.
"Now I'll catch it."

The goose heard the racket
and she, too, started hollering.
"Run-run-run downhill,
make for the woods, the woods!
They'll never-never-never
catch you in the woods."

The cocker spaniel
heard the commotion,
and he ran out from the barn
to join the chase.
Mr. Zuckerman heard,
and he came out
of the machine shed
where he was mending a tool.
Lurvy, the hired man,
heard the noise and came up
from the asparagus patch
where he was pulling weeds.

Everybody walked
toward Wilbur,
and Wilbur didn't know
what to do.
The woods seemed a long way off,
and anyway,
he had never been down there
in the woods,
and wasn't sure he would like it.

"Get around behind him, Lurvy,"
said Mr. Zuckerman,
"and drive him toward the barn!
I'll go
and get a bucket of slops."

The news of Wilbur's escape
spread rapidly
among the animals on the place.
Whenever any creature
broke loose on Zuckerman's farm,
the event was of great interest
to the others.
The goose shouted
to the nearest cow
that Wilbur was free,
and soon all the cows knew.
Then one of the cows
told one of the sheep,
and soon all the sheep knew.

The lambs learned about it
from their mothers.
The horses,
in their stalls in the barn,
pricked up their ears
when they heard
the goose hollering;
and soon the horses
had caught on
to what was happening.

"Wilbur's out," they said.
Every animal stirred
and lifted its head
and became excited to know
that one of his friends
had got free
and was no longer penned up
or tied fast.

Wilbur didn't know what to do
or which way to run.
It seemed
as though everybody
was after him.
"If this is what it's like
to be free," he thought,
"I believe
I'd rather be penned up
in my own yard."

The cocker spaniel
was sneaking up on him
from one side,
Lurvy, the hired man,
was sneaking up on him
from the other side.
Mrs. Zuckerman stood ready
to head him off
if he started for the garden,
and now Mr. Zuckerman
was coming down toward him
carrying a pail.

"This is really awful,"
thought Wilbur.
"Why doesn't Fern come?"
He began to cry.

The goose took command
and began to give orders.

"Don't just stand there!
Dodge about, Wilbur!
Dodge about!" cried the goose.
"Skip around,
run toward me,
slip in and out,
in and out, in and out!
Make for the woods!
Twist and turn!"

The cocker spaniel
sprang for Wilbur's hind leg.
Wilbur jumped and ran.
Lurvy reached out and grabbed.
Mrs. Zuckerman screamed
at Lurvy.
The goose cheered for Wilbur.
Wilbur dodged
between Lurvy's legs.
Lurvy missed Wilbur
and grabbed the spaniel
instead.

"Nicely done, nicely done!"
  cried the goose.
"Try it again, try it again!"

"Run downhill!"
  suggested the cows.

"Run toward me!"
  yelled the gander.

"Run uphill!"
  cried the sheep.

"Turn and twist!"
honked the goose.

"Jump and dance!"
said the rooster.

"Look out for Lurvy!"
called the cows.

"Look out for Zuckerman!"
yelled the gander.

"Watch out for the dog!"
cried the sheep.

"Listen to me, listen to me!"
screamed the goose.

Poor Wilbur was dazed
and frightened
by this hullabaloo.

He didn't like
being the center of all this fuss.
He tried to follow the instructions
his friends were giving him,
but he couldn't run downhill
and uphill at the same time,
and he couldn't turn and twist
when he was jumping and dancing,
and he was crying so hard
he could barely see anything
that was happening.
After all, he was a very young pig—
not much more than a baby, really.
He wished Fern was there
to take him in her arms
and comfort him.
When he looked up
and saw Mr. Zuckerman coming
with a pail of warm slops,
he felt relieved.

He lifted his nose and sniffed.
The smell was delicious—
warm milk, potato skins,
wheat middlings,
Kellogg's Corn Flakes,
and a popover left
from the Zuckermans' breakfast.

"Come, pig!" said Mr. Zuckerman,
tapping the pail. "Come pig!"

Wilbur took a step
toward the pail.

"No-no-no!" said the goose.
"It's the old pail trick, Wilbur.
Don't fall for it,
don't fall for it!
He's trying to lure you
back into captivity-ivity.
He's appealing to your stomach."

Wilbur didn't care.
The food smelled appetizing.
He took another step
toward the pail.

"Pig, pig!" said Mr. Zuckerman
in a kind voice,
and began walking slowly
toward the barnyard,

looking all about him
innocently,
as if he didn't know
that a little white pig
was following along behind him.

"You'll be sorry-sorry-sorry,"
called the goose.

Wilbur didn't care.
He kept walking
toward the pail of slops.

"You'll miss your freedom,"
honked the goose.
"An hour of freedom
is worth a barrel of slops."

Wilbur didn't care.

When Mr. Zuckerman
reached the pigpen,
he climbed over the fence
and poured the slops into the trough.
Then he pulled the loose board
away from the fence,
so that there was a wide hole
for Wilbur to walk through.

"Reconsider, reconsider!"
cried the goose.

Wilbur paid no attention.
He stepped through the fence
into his yard.
He walked to the trough
and took a long drink of slops,
sucking in the milk hungrily
and chewing the popover.
It was good to be home again.

While Wilbur ate,
Lurvy fetched a hammer
and some 8-penny nails
and nailed the board in place.
Then he and Mr. Zuckerman
leaned lazily on the fence,
and Mr. Zuckerman
scratched Wilbur's back
with a stick.

"He's quite a pig," said Lurvy.

"Yes, he'll make a good pig,"
said Mr. Zuckerman.

Wilbur heard
the words of praise.
He felt the warm milk
inside his stomach.
He felt the pleasant rubbing
of the stick along his itchy back.
He felt peaceful
and happy and sleepy.
This had been
a tiring afternoon.
It was still
only about four o'clock,
but Wilbur was ready for bed.

"I'm really too young
to go out into the world alone,"
he thought as he lay down.

A Picture for Storytelling

Courtesy Amon Carter Museum, Fort Worth, Texas

BILLY—

BILLY—

BILLY—

BILLY—

Billy Kidwell had a new ball, and Fats Martin had a new bat, so they were taking turns batting out a few on the vacant lot when Billy's mother started calling him. The first few times he pretended not to hear, but she didn't give up the way she usually did. Her voice started getting nearer and louder, so finally he shouted, "O.K.! I'm coming!"

He picked up his ball, and said gloomily, "I got to go now."

"You coming back?" asked Fats. "I can wait."

"No, I guess you better not. I got to go to that old birthday party."

"Yeah. Me, too," said Fats.

Billy brightened up. "Say, if we both go, maybe it won't be too bad. And if it is, we can duck out early."

"Before the eats?" asked Fats reproachfully. "Did you ever notice how they never drag out the ice cream and cake until the last minute, practically? Say, I bet they have it all figured out. Well, if they can hold out, so can we."

"Sure," agreed Billy. "And sometimes they have pretty neat prizes, too."

"Only I never won any yet," said Fats.

"Oh, that's a cinch, if you just have a system, like —" Billy stopped short.

"What system?" asked Fats.

"Oh, nothing. I guess I'm just lucky at games. Well, see you there."

All the time he was washing and dressing and being sent back by his mother to wash some more, Billy worried about how

A story by Marion Holland, pictures by Bill O'Day

Billy Had a System

People sometimes find themselves in a jam, just as Billy does in this story. You can decide for yourself if he handled the situation satisfactorily.

tails on things. There was always a prize, but you had to be pretty good to win it, and even if you were pretty good, somebody else was likely to come along and be better. But then, there was always a booby prize, too, for the poor dope that was the very worst.

Well, Billy just specialized in being that poor dope. Especially as he had long ago noticed that, while the first prize was apt to be something like a book or a handkerchief, the booby prize was usually something worth-while. Something that wound up and went, for instance. So he just hung back and acted sort of shy, so as to get the last turn. That way he knew just exactly how dumb he had to be to clinch the booby prize, without anybody getting suspicious. It was fool-proof, especially as there were usually so many kids milling around at a party that nobody could pay much attention to just one. He only hoped that Fats

close he had come to giving away his system to Fats. Because that was something he never intended to tell anybody, even Fats. He had figured it out for himself, almost the first time he went to a party. Just the way Fats said, you had to hang around waiting and waiting for the refreshments, and while you were waiting, there were all these games. Hunting things like jelly beans or peanuts, or guessing things, or pinning wasn't planning to keep an eye on him today, to figure out what the system was.

He almost got out of the house in his sneakers, but his mother noticed that his feet didn't sound right on the porch and called him back to put on his shoes. He was only about ten minutes late, and Fats was just going up the walk. Fats had a perfectly enormous cardboard box in both arms.

"Hey," said Billy. "What kind of a present is that, a baby elephant?"

"Present's in m' pocket," mumbled Fats, because his chin was right on top of the box and he could hardly open his mouth. "'S'n errand I got t' do. Busted china pitcher. I busted it, sort of, so I got t' take it to be mended after the party.

It was hard to shove into Peggy's house, because all the boys were hanging around in the hall, just inside the front door. Of course all the girls had walked right into the living room and were watching Peggy open presents and squealing, "Oh, how cute," and stuff like that. Only when Peggy saw the perfectly enormous package that Fats had, she rushed right up to him, all smiles, and he practically had to fight her off, while he explained that it belonged to his mother and it wasn't for her and he would get hers out of his pocket if she would please keep her shirt

on for just one minute. Anyway, pretty soon that got all straightened out, and Mrs. Crowley thoughtfully took the pitcher package out into the pantry and put it in a safe place.

Well, it was the usual sort of party. The boys wouldn't come in out of the front hall until Mrs. Crowley sat down at the piano and said they would have a quick game of "Going to Jerusalem," just to break the ice. So they had it, and it not only broke the ice, but a vase that was on the mantel and a front leg off one of the chairs. Mrs. Crowley was very polite about it and said the leg had been wobbly for a long time, anyway, but just the same, before they started the other games, she had them move most of the furniture and lamps and all out into the hall, out of the way.

Then she got a milk bottle and a spoon and a box of beans, and the game was to see who could get the most beans into the milk bottle across the room in one minute. Mrs. Crowley timed them. Billy studied this over and decided here was something he ought to be pretty good at, so he would try for first prize this time. Naturally he had to do this every so often, so nobody would catch on. When it was his turn, he scooped up the beans in the spoon and walked, fast but steady, toward the milk bottle, figuring just the right angle to tip the spoon so as not to spill any beans.

Then suddenly his toe caught in the rug, and he tripped. Beans scattered all over the room, and the four that did go in the bottle only went in by accident.

Well, there went his chance for first prize, so he decided to fall back on his system. He got another spoonful of beans, and walked extra slow and careful, just to show how hard he was trying, and this time he fell over his own foot and dropped the spoon. No beans went in the bottle.

"Too bad!" exclaimed Mrs. Crowley. "But hurry. You've got time for one more try!" So back he dashed, hurrying so hard that this time all the beans spilled off the spoon.

"Time!" called Mrs. Crowley.

Total score — four beans. He guessed that sewed up the booby prize, all right. He retired to a corner, while everybody looked sorry for him, and he tried to look sorry for himself.

Fats had the last turn. Everybody was anxious to get on to the next game, and they kept yelling at him to hurry. Well, he hurried, all right. He hurried so well that the first try, he dropped all the beans on the floor; the second try, he dropped the spoon; and the third try, he kicked over the bottle.

"Time!" called Mrs. Crowley. "Total score — zero." Everybody burst out laughing, even Fats. Everybody but Billy.

Of course, it might have been accidental. Fat people are clumsier than thin people, But Billy had never noticed Fats acting very clumsy when he was playing shortstop. It certainly looked fishy. He decided to keep an eye on Fats, and if anything like this happened again, he would certainly get him out into the kitchen and have it out with him.

The next couple of games, Billy played straight, just doing the best he could, which was pretty good, but not quite good enough. So did Fats.

Then came "Pin the Tail on the Donkey," of all the baby games. No matter how scientific and careful you were, somebody was just as like as not to win by sheer dumb luck. Billy decided it was time to give his system another try. Besides, this was probably the last game, and he hadn't won anything yet.

There were numbers on the tails. "I got eighteen," he said to Fats. "What you got?"

"Nineteen," said Fats. "Say, aren't they ever going to get around to the eats? I'm starving to death."

Well, it went along about as usual. Quite a lot of tails on the donkey picture, some on the window curtains and wall. Then Peggy's little brother, that was really too young to be there at all, only it was his sister that was having the party, got mixed up and wandered into the kitchen and pinned his tail beside the icebox. So Billy had to figure out in a hurry some place that would be even farther away, that he could get to and still act natural.

When Mrs. Crowley spun him around, he pretended to lose his balance, and staggered a little, and started off in exactly the opposite direction. There were a lot of smothered giggles, so he slowed down, and zigzagged, like somebody trying to get straightened out. And he just zigzagged out into the hall,

and pinned the tail beside the front door. Then he tore the blindfold off his eyes.

"No fair!" he hollered loudly. "You didn't start me straight!"

But everybody said, yes, it was, too, fair, so he came back, grumbling, and handed the blindfold to Mrs. Crowley.

"There," he thought. "Let's see Fats beat that!"

But Fats did. Billy could hardly believe his own eyes. Mrs.

Crowley started him off, and he wobbled a minute and fell down. Fell down right on the floor. When he got up, he started right for the hall and walked right through it and right over to the front door, which was open. And right through that and across the porch, and pinned the tail to one of the pillars.

This was too much for Billy. And his best friend, too. When Fats came back into the hall, Billy blocked his way. "Listen here," he hissed. "I know what you're doing. And you just quit, see?"

"Hey, who you shoving?" growled Fats.

"Who's shoving?" retorted Billy, giving a little shove.

Fats shoved back, a big shove. Billy skidded backwards, and lost his balance, and fell against the pile of furniture that had been moved into the hall for safety. He hit a chair, and it knocked over another chair, and that fell against one of those tippy tables

that somebody had set two lamps on and a pair of book ends and a pile of those little china ash trays. And maybe a few other things, but that was all that Billy saw out of the corner of his eye as he went down on top of the heap.

One of the girls screamed. Billy scrambled out of the wreckage,

just in time to see Fats disappear quietly through the door that led to the kitchen. By the time he got to his feet, he, too, had lost interest in what remained of the party, and he, too, passed rapidly through the empty kitchen and back pantry. Fats' box with the broken pitcher was on a pantry shelf, and, forgetting for a minute how mad he was at Fats, he reached out and grabbed it as he went by.

He took the back porch steps three at a time and was out of the yard and halfway down the alley before anyone at the party had time to figure out just what had happened. Billy turned into another alley and another, then cut across behind the Methodist Church, and ended up in the same vacant lot where he and Fats had been playing ball.

There were a lot of trees and bushes at one end of the lot, and he set the big box down and leaned back against a tree, breathing heavily. The tree seemed to be breathing heavily, too. He turned around and looked, and there was Fats on the other side of the tree.

"Now, look what you've done!" said Fats.

"What I've done!" roared Billy. "What you've done, you mean! Listen, what's the idea, chiseling in on my system, right under my very nose? You got your nerve!"

Honest bewilderment spread over Fats' round face. "I don't know what you're talking about," he said flatly. "You must be crazy."

Billy stared. "You mean you didn't do it on purpose, spill all those beans, and go way out on the porch?" he demanded.

"Now I know you're crazy," replied Fats. "What would I do that for? Say!" A great light dawned on Fats. "Is that your big system? Why, that's cheating!"

"It is not!" cried Billy angrily. "I guess I know what cheating is. It's trying to fool people into thinking you're smarter than you are. Did you ever hear of cheating to fool people into thinking you're dumber than you are?"

"Well, no," admitted Fats. "I guess you're right. Say, the next party we get invited to, maybe we could take turns using your system, huh?"

"I bet we never get invited to another party as long as we live. Either of us. After this. Not that I care," Billy added.

"Me either. Except we stayed for practically the whole party, and still we didn't get anything to eat."

"I know," groaned Billy. "Say, you forgot your box. I brought it along. Figured you wouldn't want to go back for it."

"You're crazy," retorted Fats. "I brought my box." And there it was, on the other side of the tree. They both stared at Billy's box. "Wonder what's in it," said Fats.

Billy untied the string and lifted the lid. Inside was the biggest chocolate cake he had ever seen. Of course, a good deal of icing had busted loose from being joggled while he ran. But it wasn't wasted; it was right there, stuck to the insides of the box.

"Golly," breathed Fats.

Billy tasted a piece of icing. "It isn't as if we took it on purpose," he said thoughtfully. "And besides, I suppose the party's about over, by now."

"Sure. And the others got our share of the ice cream."

"Say, that's right. Do you suppose two people could eat a whole cake?"

"They could," said Fats solemnly, "if one of them was me."

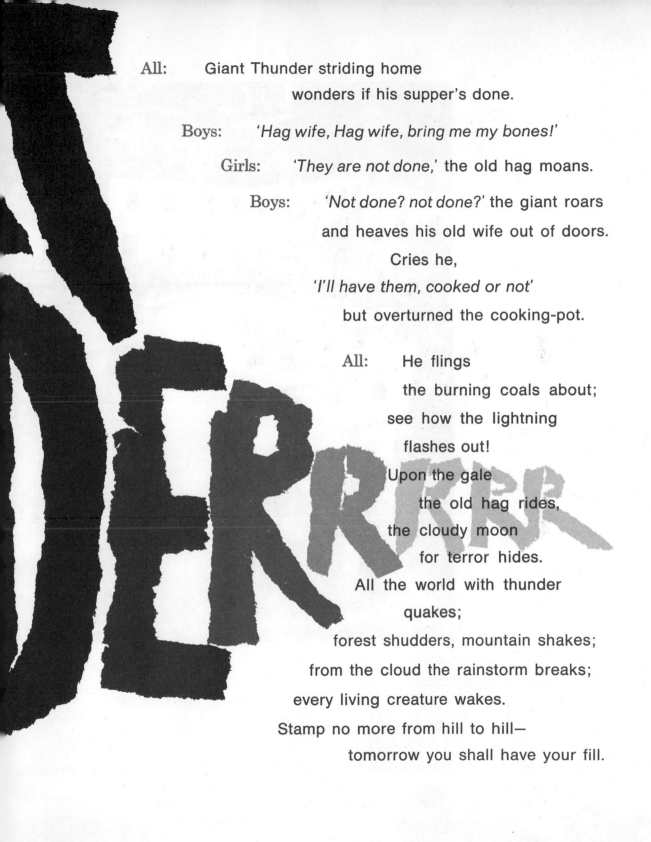

All: Giant Thunder striding home
wonders if his supper's done.

Boys: *'Hag wife, Hag wife, bring me my bones!'*

Girls: *'They are not done,'* the old hag moans.

Boys: *'Not done? not done?'* the giant roars
and heaves his old wife out of doors.
Cries he,
'I'll have them, cooked or not'
but overturned the cooking-pot.

All: He flings
the burning coals about;
see how the lightning
flashes out!
Upon the gale
the old hag rides,
the cloudy moon
for terror hides.
All the world with thunder
quakes;
forest shudders, mountain shakes;
from the cloud the rainstorm breaks;
every living creature wakes.
Stamp no more from hill to hill—
tomorrow you shall have your fill.

MARKET DAY IN ECUADOR

An article and photographs by Peter Buckley

Monday is a very important day in Ambato. Monday is market day! Thousands of people come to this market, from the city itself and from far away, by foot, by bus, and on horseback. There are no supermarkets in Ambato, and there are very few stores. The marketplace is the one place to go if you want to buy or sell.

Ambato is almost two miles high in the Andes Mountains. It is always cool there, even though it is very near the equator. On either side of Ambato, the mountains drop down quickly to the hot tropic lowlands.

Far below Ambato, in the tropics, certain Indian tribes grow sugar. On Sunday they wrap some of their sugar in palm leaves and set out for the marketplace in Ambato to be ready for sale day, Monday.

Other Indian tribes come to the marketplace with rope to sell. The rope is made from grass which grows wild, in fields near their villages in the lowlands. The Indians labor long and hard to make the rope.

Indians of a tribe that raises cattle are trying to sell their cows.

Not far from them is the part of the market where horses are sold.

Sugar, rope, cows, horses: you can buy almost anything you want on Monday in Ambato. The market spreads out from the central square until it almost fills the city streets. There is a special place for every item, and everyone knows exactly where to go if he wants to sell a needle or if he wants to buy a bag of corn.

Many Indian languages are spoken in the market because each tribe has its own language. Everyone, however, speaks a little Spanish, and so it is easy for a man from one tribe to speak to a man from another tribe, even though their own languages may be different.

The market is a very important place. It is important not just because it is like a giant department store and

a giant supermarket put together so that people can buy and sell what they need, but it is important because people talk to each other.

They tell each other the news from the villages, their farms, their towns. Many men and many women with their babies firmly strapped to their backs come to the market to learn the news.

There are no newspapers in the villages or on the farms far from the city; and even if there were, they would be useless because many people cannot read. Instead of reading the news, the people gather together in the market on Monday.

When they are through with their business, the people of one tribe meet with the people of another tribe.

The news is very important. One man who raises sheep hears that floods in a distant valley have drowned many large flocks of sheep.

Knowing this, the sheep-farmer realizes that during the next year there will be a shortage of sheep in the market, and so he will be able to raise his prices when he brings his own sheep for sale.

An Indian boy, who has four sheep and a pig, each tied to the end of a rope, gets into trouble when the five animals decide to go in different directions.

Men from the Otavalo Tribe who live on the shores of a lake more than a hundred miles north of Ambato meet every Monday at the market.

A father learns that his son is no longer busy transporting bananas but, instead, is growing his own bananas.

People hear about their friends who have gotten married, a new baby and distant relatives who have died.

They hear about a new tractor, a better way to plow a field, a new hospital where they can take a sick child for free medical care and a good movie playing in Ambato.

A man who needs a job will ask for one in the market.

A man who wants to buy a house will ask if anyone knows of a good one for sale.

A man with a broken motor will ask where he can get it fixed.

A woman who is ill will ask for a doctor.

There is no end to the news you can hear on a Monday in Ambato.

A day at the market is busy from beginning to end. After hours of talk, friends who have not met for weeks eat together.

Then everyone has to think of going home. Some must catch a bus for the tropical lowlands. Others ride their horses to farms high in the cold mountains. The people who live in Ambato walk slowly home. In another week it will be market day once again in Ambato.

Late in the afternoon a farmer puts his son on the new donkey he has bought at the market, and together they start for home.

THE *Beat* OF MY HEART

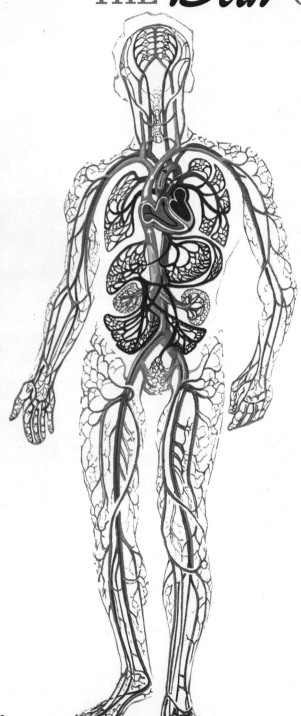

An essay by Maryhelen Vannier,
pictures by Pauline M. Larivière
and Mel Hunter

Lub-dup...
 Lub-dup...
  Lub-dup...
   This strange sound
    is the sound
     of a wonderful machine
      inside your body.
      It is the sound
       of your heart beating.
      Your heart is a pump
      which will never
      stop working
      as long as you live,
     but it can rest
      even while it is working.
    Your heart
    is a hollow muscle
   divided into four parts.
   It is about the size
   of your fist.
   As you grow,
   it too will grow in size.

To find out
where your heart is,
put your right hand
in the middle
of the left side of your chest.
Now move your fingers around
until you find
the spot where
the heartbeat is strongest.
Your hand is now
pointing to your heart.
Listen to the heartbeat
of a friend
by putting your ear
to his chest.
To hear the sound even better,
hold an empty mailing tube
or a rolled-up piece
of heavy paper
to your friend's heart.
When the heart goes *lub*,
it is drawing in blood.
When it goes *dup*,
it is pushing blood out
to all parts of the body.
Your heart has
this most important job to do—
pumping blood
to all parts of your body.

Blood feeds
all the cells and organs
of your body
so that they can do
their own special work
to keep you physically fit.
Your heart pumps blood
from your head
to your toes,
to your liver
and your lungs.
Just as a wheel
can turn slowly or fast,
your heart can work
at a slow or a fast pace.
If you want to see
how your heart changes quickly
from working at a slow pace
to working at a faster pace,
try this.
First listen
to a friend's heartbeat
and count the number of beats
in a minute.
Now ask your friend
to run fast
for about a minute.
Then listen to his heart again.
How many times a minute
is his heart beating now?

How can you best take care
of the motor that you feel pumping inside your body?
This article suggests two things you can do.
It also invites you to explore
the mysterious sound and rhythm of that motor.

lub-dup
lub-dup
lub-dup
lub-dup
lub-dup
lub-dup
lub-dup
lub-dup
lub-dup
lub-dup
lub-dup
lub-dup
lub-dup
lub-dup
lub-dup
lub-dup
lub-dup
lub-dup
lub-dup
lub-dup
lub-dup
lub-dup
lub-dup

Count his heartbeats again
after he has rested
for a minute.
By comparing the number
of heartbeats
under these different conditions,
you will discover that
the heart is
a sensitive machine
working inside the body.

You can test this fact again
by checking your own heartbeat.
Place three fingertips
of your right hand
on the inside of your left wrist.
You will feel the beat
of your heart.
This is called your pulse.
Count the number of times
your heart beats in a minute.

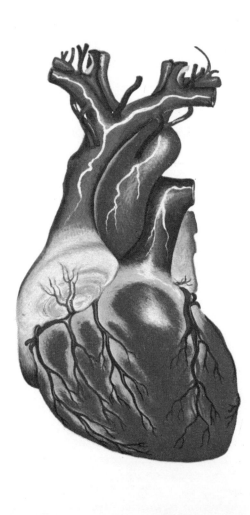

Now, run for a minute
and count the heartbeats
in your pulse again.
Lie down and rest for a minute,
and then count once more.
See how exercise makes
your heart work
harder and faster?
Exercise helps your heart
to become stronger
and to be able
to do its work better.
Your heart beats
as long as you live.
It rests for 1/6 of a second
between every beat.
When you are asleep or resting,
your heart beats
at a slower rate.
This rest gives your heart
a chance to keep
in good working condition
as well as to grow
bigger and stronger.

Since you are becoming
taller and heavier
every school year,
your heart must grow larger, too.
Your bigger body needs
a bigger motor to keep it
in good working order.
There are many ways
to take care of your heart,
but the two best ones are
the easiest to do.
One is to get lots of exercise
by playing vigorous games
out of doors.
Play games that have lots
of running and jumping,
or hitting and kicking balls.
The other way
to take care of your heart
is to be sure you get
at least ten hours of sleep
every night
and do restful things
from time to time
throughout the day.
On and on your heart beats—
year in and year out.
Lub-dup...
Lub-dup...
Lub-dup...

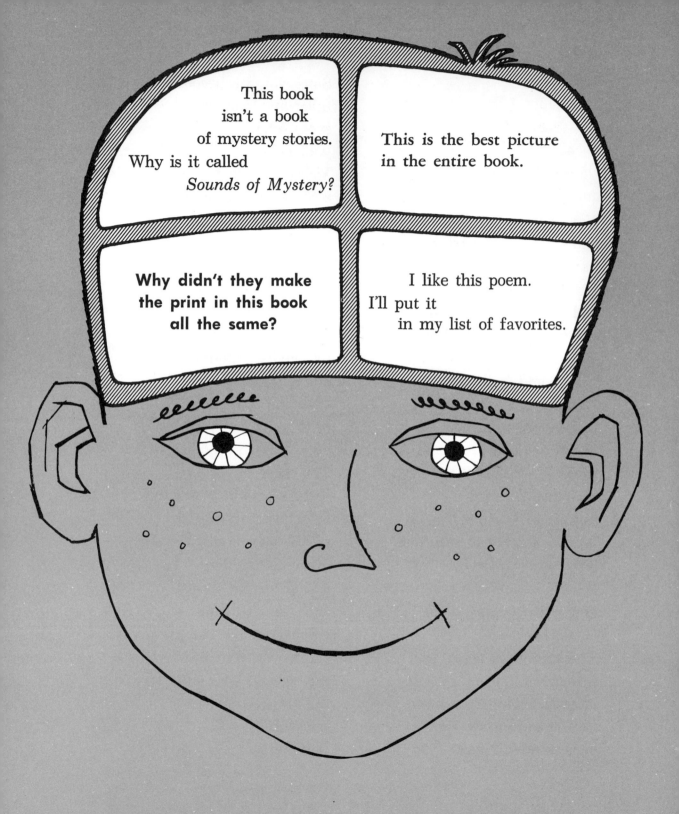

This book
isn't a book
of mystery stories.
Why is it called
Sounds of Mystery?

This is the best picture
in the entire book.

**Why didn't they make
the print in this book
all the same?**

I like this poem.
I'll put it
in my list of favorites.

viewing the printed page

Ever since I began reading,
I have been making choices
about what I read—
choices about the pictures
and ideas
and kinds of writing I've found
on the "printed page."
I have liked some
of what I've read.
I have rejected
much of what I've read.
But the process
of choosing what pleases me
started years and years ago
when I was very young.

I still get a feeling of joy
when I open a new book,
when I come unexpectedly
upon a poem in a magazine,
when I see an advertisement
that uses styles of lettering
and words and pictures
that are pleasing
to the eye and ear,
and when I find a painting
or a photograph
that seems to tell me
more than words can say.

Through the years
I've discovered some books so good,
that they became lifetime favorites.
These are books that I have read
over and over again.

My first "great" book
was *The Brownies*,
written and illustrated by Palmer Coxe.
I read it the first time
when I was about
five or six years old.
I couldn't read the words then
(and later, when I was able to,
I didn't like the stories),
but, oh, how I liked the pages
and pages of drawings:
Brownies swarming over a ship,
Brownies invading a ballpark
    at night,
Brownies slipping into a circus,
Brownies trying to milk a cow.

I've learned since that many books
are worthwhile only because
of the pictures, and that pictures
often tell more than words.
Enjoying a book because of its pictures
is one way to enjoy reading.

as an art experience

An essay by Bill Martin, Jr.,
illustration by Frank Aloise

And then there was poetry.
My mother often read aloud to us children
as she stood at the ironing board doing up the overalls and shirts
for a large family of boys.
And my teachers, too, took time to read poems aloud.
Soon I was saying the poetry "by heart"
and learning to read it on my own.

Wee Willie Winkie runs through the town,
Upstairs and downstairs
In his nightgown.

Over in the meadow in the sand in the sun,
Lived an old mother turtle and her little turtle one.

Sing hey! Sing hey! for Christmas day,
Twine mistletoe and holly,
Our friendship grows with winter snows
So let us all be jolly!

It was the schooner Hesperus
That sailed the wintry sea,
And the skipper had taken his little daughter
To bear him company.

How does the water come down at Lodore?
My little boy asked me thus
once on a time
And, moreover, he tasked me to tell him in rhyme. . . .
So I told him in rhyme,
for, of rhyme I had store.
And 'twas my vocation, so should I sing,
For I was laureate to them and the King.

What a pleasure it was
to hear the resounding sounds
    of poetry,
to "drink in" what I liked,
and to know
that I didn't have to like
all of it.

I also found lots of books
that were worth reading:
The Little Red Hen,
Puss in Boots,
The Dutch Twins,
The Rover Boys,
Dog of Flanders,
Treasure Island,
The Jungle Book,
Seven League Boots,
and many many others.
These books helped me discover
the joy and feeling of power
in being able to make
printed words come alive
as people and animals
on great adventures.
At the same time,
I found that listening to a story
could be just as satisfying
as reading a story.

My mother and my brothers
and my teachers
read many books aloud to me,
and I began to find favorites
that I wanted to hear
over and over:
The Teeny-Weeny Woman,
When We Were Very Young,
Willie Do and Willie Don't,
The Goops,
The Enchanted Garden,
The Wizard of Oz,
Call of the Wild,
Smoky, The Story of a Cow Horse.

And in high school,
I was lucky enough
to have a teacher who read aloud
the classic play of *Macbeth*
by William Shakespeare,
and I've never forgotten
the powerful story
and its beautiful language.
Once I had heard a story
read aloud,
that story was apt to be
my next choice of a library book
to see if I could read it
by myself.
And so it was with *Macbeth.*
I've been reading it ever since.

In those days,
there weren't many pictures
in our books,
and what there were
usually were in black and white.
But my grandmother subscribed
to ten or twenty
magazines and catalogs
filled with colorful pictures,
and I "picture-read" them all
from cover to cover,
pondering the meanings
of being a sailor in a shipwreck,
of being a cowboy herding cattle,
of being a hunter lost
on a cold winter's night,
of being a boy swinging
in an apple tree,
of being a captive
looking straight down the barrel
of some desperado's gun.
I soon began making choices
of pictures I did and didn't like.
I even had my favorite
        calendar pictures
from among the wide variety
of free calendars
we collected from the stores
in our little town.

And, oh,
the joy of finding sentences
that fell in pleasant
and logical patterns!
Much of the language
that I liked
didn't seem to make sense,
but that didn't matter.
It was the sound
and majesty of sentences
that counted:

Once in high and far-off times,
the elephant, O best beloved,
had no trunk.

"Not I," said the cat.
"Not I," said the dog.
"Not I," said the pig.
"Then I will," said the little red hen,
and so she did.

Papers! Papers! Daily papers!
Which one will you choose?
From Detroit and Chicago.
From New York and San Francisco.
Right here for the daily news.

And they lived happily ever after.

Over the river and through the woods
To grandmother's house we go.

Thine alabaster cities gleam
undimmed by human tears.

Tune in tomorrow
for further adventures
of *Little Orphan Annie.*

*How the snowflakes
enfolded them gently
as did the robins
the babes in the woods.*

As I pondered
these continuing experiences
with stories and poems,
with books and magazines
    and radio,
with drawings and paintings
    and photographs,
with language
    and the sounds of language,
I continued to make choices
of likes and dislikes.
I am still making those choices
    today.

This is what happens
when you view the printed page
as art experience.
It helps you look at the world
through the eyes of someone else—
the author, the poet, the painter,
or a character in the story.

By momentarily becoming
that or this person
and trying to think as he thinks
and feel as he feels,
you find yourself
thinking and feeling
in ways that you haven't thought
and felt before.
And then you can decide
whether or not you liked
these new thoughts and feelings.

Sounds of Mystery
is especially planned
to help you explore your taste
in language and art
    and literature.
It offers a wide variety of choices.
On the next page is the song
"Somewhere over the Rainbow."
Do you like the way
it has been designed for reading?
Do you like
the thoughts and feelings
it engenders?
Would you choose it
as one of your favorite selections
in this book?

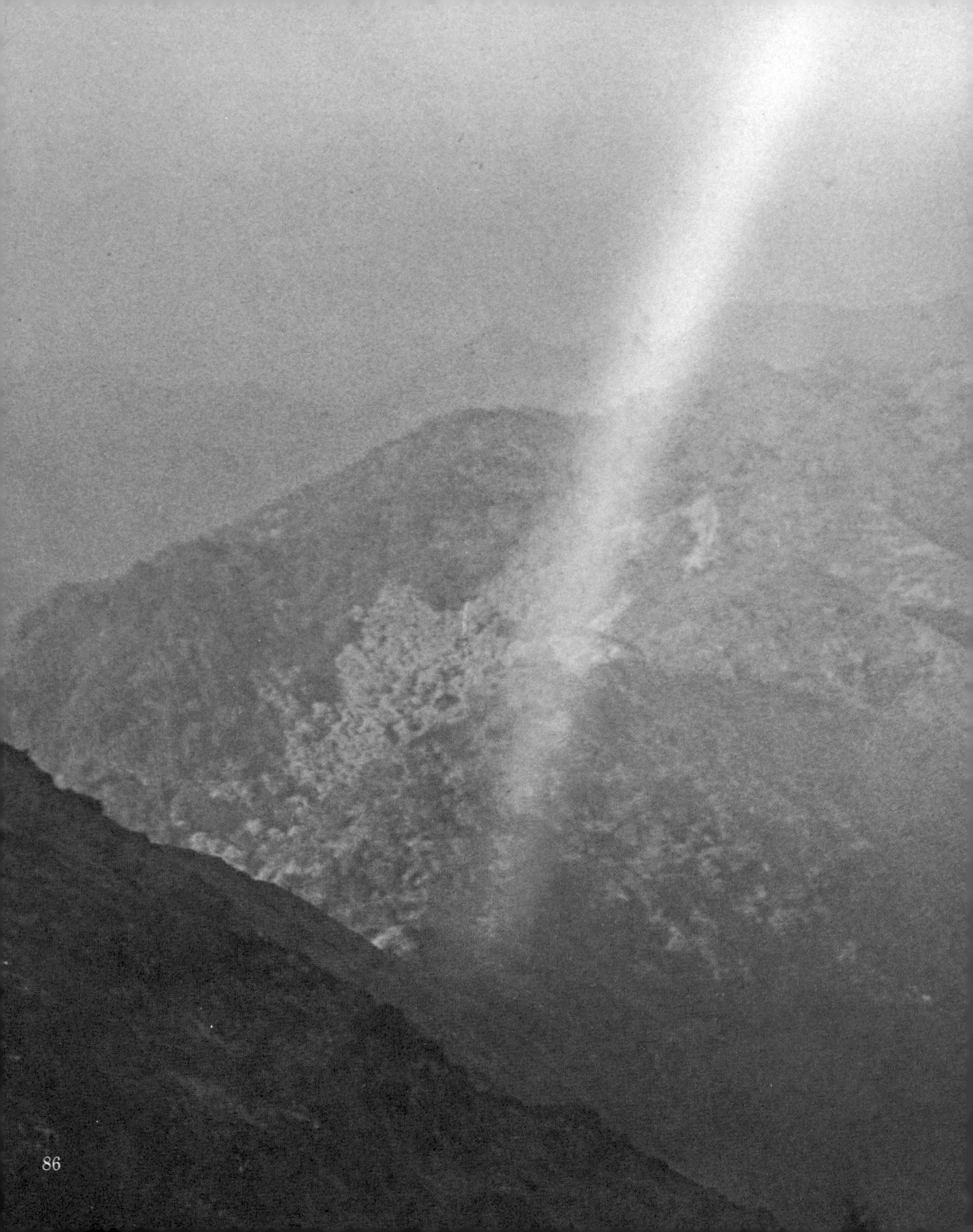

Somewhere over the Rainbow

Somewhere over the rainbow
    way up high,
There's a land that I heard of
    once in a lullaby.
Somewhere over the rainbow
    skies are blue,
And the dreams that you dare to dream
    really do come true.

Someday I'll wish upon a star
    and wake up
Where the clouds are far behind me,
Where troubles melt like lemon drops,
    away, above the chimney tops
That's where you'll find me.

Somewhere over the rainbow
    bluebirds fly,
Birds fly over the rainbow,
    why then, oh why can't I?
If happy little bluebirds fly
    beyond the rainbow,
Why oh why can't I?

A song by E. Y. Harburg,
photograph by Werner Stoy,
Camera Hawaii

BUT TOADS DON'T BITE

A dialogue by William Saroyan,
pictures by John Burningham

My uncle and I got out of the Ford roadster

in the middle of his land

and began to walk over the dry earth.

This land is my land, he said.

He walked slowly, kicking into the dry soil.

A HORNED TOAD SCRAMBLED

over the earth
at my uncle's feet.
My uncle
clutched my shoulder
and came to a pious halt.
What is that animal?
  he said.
That little tiny lizard?
  I said.
That mouse with horns.
What is it?
  my uncle said.
I don't know for sure.
We call them horny toads,
  I said.
The horned toad
came to a halt
about three feet away
and turned its head.

My uncle looked down
at the small animal.
Is it poison?
  he said.
To eat?
Or if it bites you?
  I said.
Either way,
  my uncle said.
I don't think
it's good to eat.
I think it's harmless.
I've caught many of them.
They grow sad in captivity,
but never bite.

Shall I catch this one?
  I said.
Please do,
  my uncle said.
I sneaked up
on the horned toad,
then sprang on it
while my uncle looked on.
Careful!
Are you sure it isn't poison?
  he said.
I've caught many of them,
  I said.
I took the horned toad
to my uncle.
He tried not to seem afraid.
A lovely little thing,
isn't it?
  he said.
His voice was unsteady.

Would you like to hold it?
  I said.
No, you hold it.
I have never before been so close
to such a thing as this.
I see it has eyes.
I suppose it can see us,
  my uncle said.
I suppose it can.
It's looking up at you now,
  I said.
My uncle looked the horned toad
straight in the eye.
The horned toad looked my uncle
straight in the eye.
For fully half a minute
they looked one another
straight in the eye
and then the horned toad
turned its head aside
and looked down at the ground.
My uncle sighed with relief.

They never travel
in great numbers.
You hardly ever see
more than one at a time,
  I said.
A big one
could probably bite
a man to death,
  my uncle said.
They don't grow big.
This is as big as they grow,
  I said.
They seem to have an awful eye
for such small creatures.
Are you sure they don't mind
being picked up?
  my uncle said.

A THOUSAND OF THEM COULD KILL A MAN I SUPPOSE,

he said.

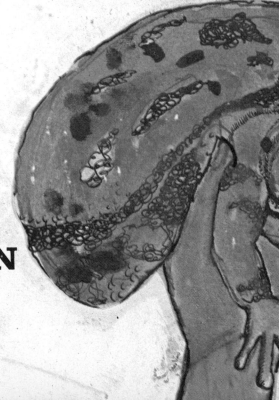

I suppose they forget
all about it the minute
you put them down,
  I said.
Do you really think so?
  my uncle said.
I don't think
they have very good memories,
  I said.
My uncle straightened up,
breathing deeply.
  He said,
Put the little creature down.
Let us not be cruel
to the innocent creations
of Almighty God.
If it is not poison
and grows no larger
than a mouse
and does not travel
in great numbers
and has no memory
to speak of,
let the timid little thing
return to the earth.
Let us be gentle
toward
these small things
which live
on the earth
with us.

Yes, sir,
    I said.
I placed the horned toad
on the ground.
Gently now.
Let no harm come
to this strange dweller
on my land,
    my uncle said.
The horned toad
scrambled away.
These little things
have been living on soil
of this kind for centuries,
    I said.

Centuries?
Are you sure?
  my uncle said.
I'm not sure,
but I imagine they have.
They're still here, anyway,
  I said.
My uncle looked around
at his land,
at the cactus
and brush growing out of it,
at the sky overhead.

What have they been eating
all this time?
  he shouted.
I don't know,
  I said.
What would you say
they've been eating?
  he said.
Insects, I guess.
Insects?
What sort of insects?
  my uncle shouted.
Little bugs, most likely,
  I said.
I don't know their names.
I can find out tomorrow at school.

A bat is born
     naked and blind and pale.
His mother makes a pocket of her tail
     and catches him.
He clings to her long fur
     by his thumbs and toes and teeth.
And then the mother dances through the night,
     doubling and looping,
     soaring, somersaulting —
     her baby hangs on underneath.
All night, in happiness, she hunts and flies.
Her sharp cries
     like shining needlepoints of sound
     go out into the night and,
     echoing back,
     tell her what they have touched.
She hears how far it is,
     how big it is,
     which way it's going:
     she lives by hearing.
The mother eats the moths and gnats she catches
     in full flight;

in full flight
the mother drinks the water of the pond
she skims across.
Her baby hangs on tight.
Her baby drinks the milk she makes him
in moonlight or starlight, in mid-air.
Their single shadow,
printed on the moon
or fluttering across the stars,
whirls on all night;
at daybreak
the tired mother flaps home to her rafter.
The others all are there.
They hang themselves up by their toes,
they wrap themselves in their brown wings.
Bunched upside down,
they sleep in air.
Their sharp ears,
their sharp teeth,
their quick sharp faces
are dull and slow and mild.
All the bright day, as the mother sleeps,
she folds her wings
about her sleeping child.

A poem by Randall Jarrell,
drawing by Maurice Sendak

language works
in
chunks
of meaning

Sentences in most books are written across the column like this:

Sometimes the male lions may help ambush the game, but more often they take their rest under shady trees and watch while the lionesses stalk and kill the game that will become a feast for all of the lions.

You may have noticed, however, that many sentences
in this book are not printed that way.
They have been broken apart
into special groups of words, like this:

Sometimes the male lions
may help ambush the game,
but more often
they take their rest
under shady trees
and watch
while the lionesses
stalk and kill the game
that will become a feast
for all of the lions.

Each of these groups of words has a meaning
that is more important than any single word
within the group. The words in a group,
therefore, must be read together as a subset,
and all of the subsets are read together
to make the more important set, the sentence.
This is the way our language works.

An essay by Bill Martin, Jr.

An experienced reader does not move through a sentence
by reading each word separately. He learns to see
(and to sense) in groupings of words that best create meaning.

When a sentence is written from margin to margin
across a column or a page, with no special emphasis
on the chunks of meaning (grouping of words),
the reader must do the work of seeing the sentence
in chunks of sense (or meaning).
This is not always an easy task.

In this book, we have broken many of the sentences into chunks
to help you train your eyes
to read sentences this way.
It is a faster and better way to read.

Now, for a little practice in looking for chunks
of meaning within sentences, try reading this telegram
which has no punctuation.
How can you best group the words
to make sense out of what is being said?

THANKS FOR YOUR TELEGRAM TELLING
US WHEN YOU WILL ARRIVE IN KANSAS
CITY WE WILL BE AT THE TRAIN TO
MEET YOU WHATEVER PLANS YOU MAKE
FOR THE PICNIC WILL SUIT US WE CAN
GO EITHER MONDAY OR TUESDAY
LOVE AUNT EMMA

What happens to the meaning if you read the first five words,
Thanks for your telegram telling,
as a chunk? What happens to the meaning
if you read each word separately with no relationship to other words?

Now let's look at another sentence that has been broken down
into its chunks of meaning:

1) The next afternoon
2) Sara and her mother
3) were frosting cookies
4) in the kitchen,
5) and Tim
6) was putting the wreath up
7) on the front door.

You may question whether or not chunks 2 and 3
and chunks 5 and 6 should be combined into one.
That's how it is when you read a sentence in chunks.
Different people will select different groupings.
The only thing that matters is, does the grouping make sense?
Notice what would happen if you regrouped 5 and 6 like this:

5) and Tim was putting
6) the wreath up

This arrangement doesn't work
because *the wreath up* doesn't make sense.
Meaning is the key in deciding which words chunk together.

Isn't it interesting that some chunks of meaning
can be moved about in the sentence
without changing the meaning. For example,
in how many different ways can you arrange the seven chunks
without destroying the sentence meaning?

A good reader accustoms his eyes to seeing chunks of meaning
as he moves through a sentence.
A good writer thinks in chunks of meaning
as he puts his sentences on paper.
Perhaps you'd like to try this idea out
to improve your own reading and writing.

Have you noticed that poets tend to arrange their poems
in ways that make the chunks of meaning stand out?

Why did the children put beans in their ears

when the one thing we told the children
they must not do
was put beans in their ears?

Why did the children
pour molasses on the cat
when the one thing we told the children
they must not do
was pour molasses on the cat?

A poem by Carl Sandburg

Now—here are three fables on the following pages,
each printed in a different style.
"The Milkmaid and Her Pail" is printed in chunks of meaning.
"The Dog and the Shadow" is printed in narrow columns
from margin to margin.
"The Donkey and the Salt" is printed in a wide column
from margin to margin.
Which way of arranging the sentences do you like best?

The Milkmaid and Her Pail

A farmer's daughter had been
out to milk the cows,
and was returning home
carrying her pail of milk
upon her head.
As she walked along,
she fell a-musing
after this fashion:
"The milk in this pail
will provide me with cream,
which I will make into butter
and take to market to sell.
With the money
I will buy a number of eggs,
and these, when hatched,
will produce chickens,
and by and by I shall have
a large poultry-yard.
Then I shall sell
some of my chickens,
and with the money
which they will bring in
I will buy myself a new gown,
which I shall wear
when I go to the fair;
and all the young fellows
will admire it
and come and make love to me,
but I shall toss my head
and have nothing to say to them."

Forgetting all about the pail,
she tossed her head haughtily.
Down went the pail.
The milk was spilled,
and all her fine castles in the air
vanished in a moment!

Do not count your chickens before they are hatched.

The Dog and the Shadow

It happened that a dog had got a piece of meat and was carrying it home in his mouth to eat it in peace. Now on his way home, he had to cross a plank lying across a running brook. As he crossed, he looked down and saw his own shadow reflected in the water beneath. Thinking it was another dog with another piece of meat, he made up his mind to have that meat also. So he made a snap at the shadow in the water, but as he opened his mouth, his piece of meat fell from his mouth, dropped into the water and was never more seen.

Beware lest you lose what you have by grasping at a shadow.

Fables by Aesop,
linoleum cuts by Eric Carle

The Donkey and the Salt

A merchant once loaded his donkey with some bags of salt and was driving her to town, when she slipped and fell into the water as they were crossing a plank over a small stream. The donkey swam to shore, but the salt was all dissolved and streamed out of the bags, so that the donkey had a light load the rest of the way. The next day, the donkey managed to slip at the same spot with the load of salt, and again walked to town with a light burden.

The merchant figured out the donkey's trick and decided to teach her a lesson.

The next day he loaded her down with a great pile of sponges. The foolish donkey again slipped at the crossing, but this time she could hardly drag herself out of the water with the soaking sponges and staggered into town under a tremendous load.

Fools always play the same trick once too often.

I am he, who, when I chwose,
prefers those things involving twos:
twomorrows,
and twodays,
blwo jays,
and twosdays,
two-twobes-for-the-price-of-one twothpaste,
and friends whwo are never, never two-faced,
bicycle twobes
and singable twones,
garden twols
and sweet dark prwones,
so if I lwos one of the twos
another is on hand to uwos.

A response by Bill Martin, Jr.

Why are lots of things in twos?
Hands on clocks,
and gloves,
and shoes,
scissor-blades,
and water-taps,
collar studs,
and luggage straps,
walnut shells,
and pigeons' eggs,
arms
and eyes
and ears
and legs —
will you kindly tell me who's
so fond of making things in twos?

A poem by John Drinkwater

BEES

A true story by Gene Fulks, pictures by Zena Bernstein

It is early in the morning.
The bees are waking up.
Flights of worker bees are swarming
out of the beehive...
up, up,
over the tree,
over the meadows,
over the fields of clover,
across the river,
straight to the orange grove,
far, far away.
They fly so far away from the beehive,
so far away from home,
oh, how will they find their long way back?

Buzz...buzz...buzz.
Thousands of worker bees
swarm down into the orange trees,
swarm down into the sweetness
of the sweet white orange blossoms.
Burrowing deep into the blossoms,
they gather the sweet nectar
and buzz from blossom to blossom.
Their honey sacs, now filled with nectar,
their pollen baskets bulging with golden pollen,
the worker bees fly homeward,
carrying their heavy loads.

With eyes as keen as the eyes of a bird,
they see the bend in the river,
they see the fence through the clover,
they see the tree in the meadow,
and they see the narrow little lane
that leads them back to the beehive.
The worker bees never get lost.
The worker bees always come home.

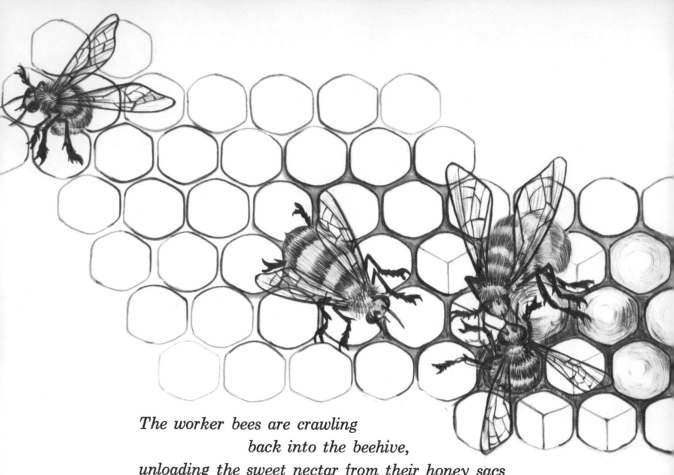

The worker bees are crawling
          back into the beehive,
unloading the sweet nectar from their honey sacs
and the golden pollen from their pollen baskets.
Most of the worker bees are ready to go
     to the orange grove again,
but some will not return.
Weary with work,
their wings tattered and torn,
some drop to the floor of the hive and die.
But the work goes on.
Other worker bees take their places
and swarm out of the beehive
     to fly toward the orange grove.
The endless search for nectar and golden pollen
     goes on and on and on.

But back inside the beehive,
thousands of other worker bees
are swarming over the honeycomb,
turning the nectar from the orange
    blossoms into honey,
chewing the golden pollen to feed the baby bees,
making wax from some of the nectar
    to build the honeycomb,
buzz...buzz...buzzing.
So many bees you couldn't count them all,
all of them busy from morning till dark—
all except the drone bees.

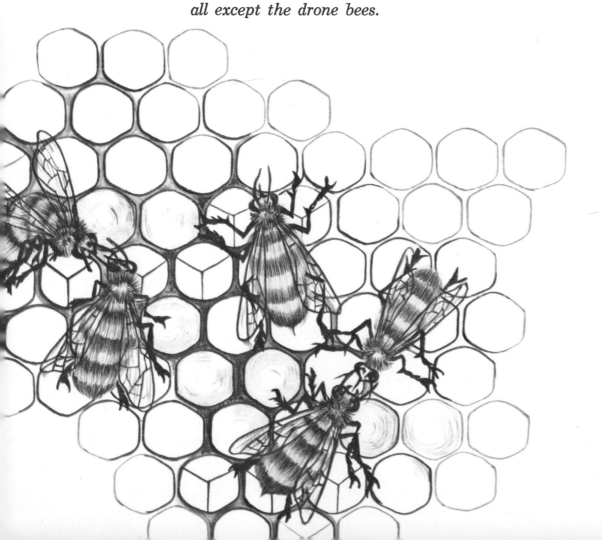

The drone bees are men bees.
They keep the queen bee company.
They dawdle around the beehive,
begging the busy nurse bees for droplets of honey,
 pestering,
 begging
 and buzzing
 all day long.
One of the drone bees
will one day mate with the queen bee
and become the father of new baby bees.
The queen bee is the largest bee.
She is the queen of the beehive.
From morning till night,
after she has mated,
she crawls over the honeycomb
laying eggs to hatch baby bees.
The queen bee is a busy bee.
She sometimes lays 4,000 eggs in a day,
4,000 eggs...4,000 baby bees.

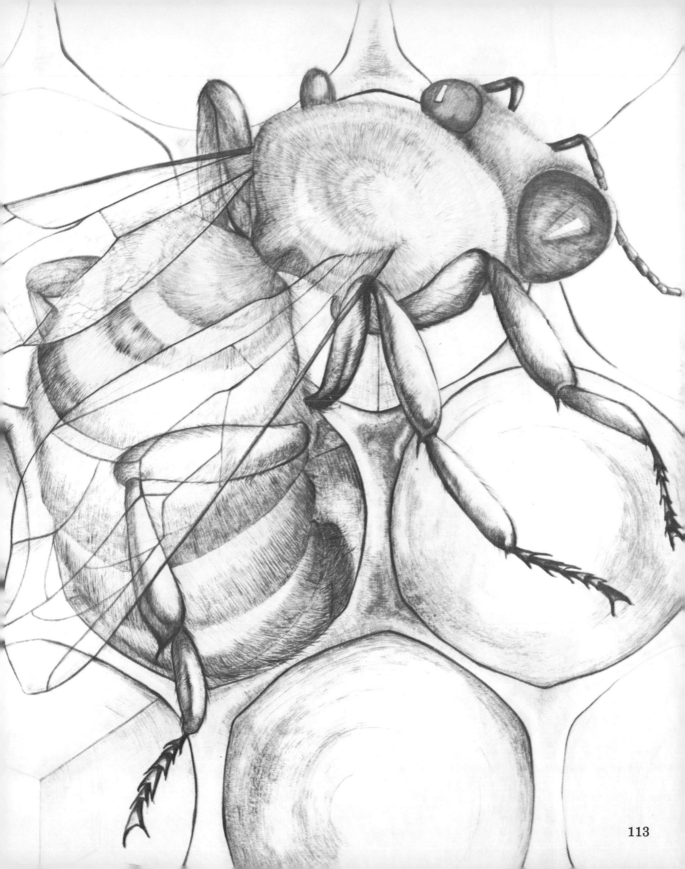

A beekeeper is coming down the narrow lane.
He wears heavy gloves and a netting over his hat.
He is coming to rob the beehive of its
        rich golden honey.
Step...step...step.
The beekeeper is walking away
with a bucketful
        of rich golden honey.
And still there comes another intruder.
Scratch...scratch...scratch.
A mother skunk and her four kittens
        come to the beehive.
They come at night
when the bees cannot fly and sting them.
Oh how wise, Mother Skunk!
Scratch...scratch...scratch.
The bees stir but they do not fly.
They do not fly at night
because they cannot see
        their way in the dark.
The bees, sensing the danger,
        crawl out of the beehive
        to see who is there.
Snap...snap...snap.
The skunks eat bees until they are full.

But soon it will be morning.
And soon there will be more nectar
    and more honey
    and more eggs
    and more bees.
The endless making of honey
goes on and on and on.

Dr. Trick

Hello,
I'm a magician.
Now watch closely!
I shall cut Miss Partly into two parts.
In this case, the hand
   is not quicker than the eye,
because I'm using a saw.

Cut! Cut! Cut!

I'm cutting Miss Partly in two.

A monologue by Henry W. Ford,
pictures by Bob Shein

THE TWO PARTS OF PARTLY
ARE NOT EXACTLY HALVES.

And here she is,
    Miss Bonnie Partly,
in two parts, but not in halves.
Thank you for your generous
                    applause!

*Not all arithmetic lessons look alike. Here is one that will
tickle your funny bone at the same time that it provokes you
into dealing with fractions and proportions.*

And now,
I shall attempt that once-in-a-lifetime,
butcher-boy rope trick
which I learned from a tattooed sailor in Siam.

Hocus-pocus,
Jimmy Kaknowkus,
watch closely
for
what you can't see!

Halve the whole,
then halve one of the halves,
then halve one quarter,
halve that half,
then halve the last half,
and what do you have?

THE SMALLER
THE PART,
THE BIGGER
THE NUMBER.

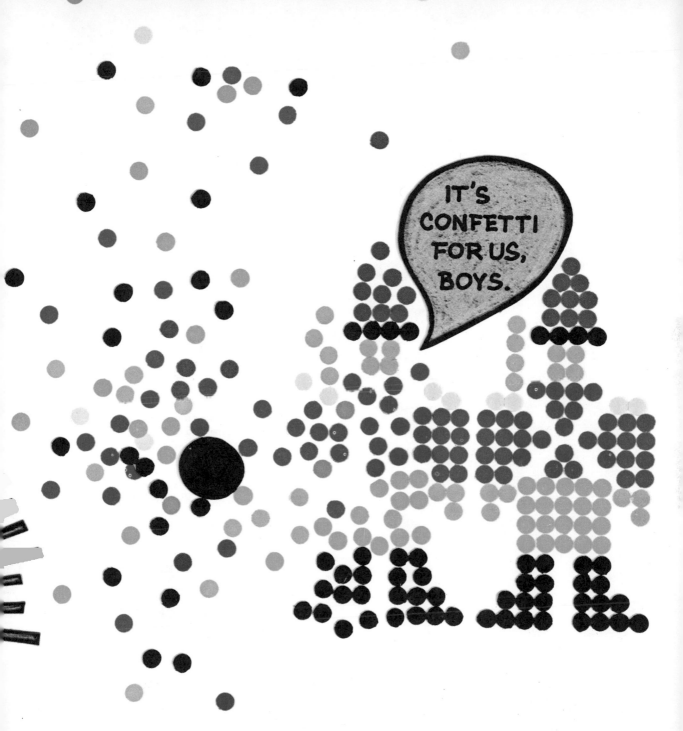

Rabbits tend to be favorite characters
in talking-animal stories.
The talking rabbit in this story
is George,
and surprisingly enough,
the story may convince you
that it's quite natural
for a rabbit
to talk with people.

GEORGE

A chapter from the novel, *George,*
by Agnes Sligh Turnbull
with pictures by Betty Fraser

Mrs. Weaver awakened that morning
with a bad headache.
She managed
to get down to the kitchen
in her dressing gown
and prepare breakfast for Mr. Weaver,
who always had to catch a train
for the city,
and for Milly and Tommy,
who had to be at school
by a quarter of nine.

When they were all gone,
she made some
peanut butter and jelly sandwiches
which she wrapped in waxed paper
and left on the table
for the children's lunch
in case she wasn't able
to come downstairs again.
She knew
Milly could get the milk
out of the icebox
and the cookies from the jar.
Milly was very capable.

Tommy had to be watched
for fear
he would make his whole lunch
on cookies
and forget his sandwiches.
When she had finished her work,
she went slowly upstairs
and lay down again in bed.
Her head hurt her very much.

For a good while
the house was perfectly quiet;
then she began to hear something.
It seemed
like soft little velvet pat-pats
on the stairs.
At first
she thought it was the throbbing
in her head she heard;

then the small strange sounds
grew a bit louder
in the upper hall
and stopped.
Very slowly she opened her eyes.
There in the doorway
sat a brown rabbit.
It appeared to be
like any other good-sized rabbit
she had ever seen
except that this one wore glasses.
He looked at her
and bowed slightly.

"Name is George," he said.
"George H.
Since everyone asks
what the H stands for,
I'll tell you right away.
Stands for Hare.
My grandfather
was a Belgian Hare.
Very fine family."

"How did you get in?"
Mrs. Weaver asked faintly.

"Kitchen screen.
Tommy left it open.
As usual."

"You know Tommy?"

"Of course.
I've spent a good deal of time
in your garden."

Mrs. Weaver's eyes opened wider.
"Then it's you
who has been eating
my young lettuce?"

"Now, now!" said George,
adjusting his glasses
since the twitching of his nose
made them slide down a little.
"I hoped that matter
wouldn't come up.
I admit I may have nibbled,
but only the edges.
To change the subject,
what seems to be the matter
with you?"

"A headache," she moaned.
"It's very severe!"

"Oh, if that's all,
I can cure it.
Don't be startled.
I'm coming up on the bed."

With one big leap
he settled himself
close to Mrs. Weaver.
"If you'll excuse my back,"
he said,
"I'll sit here
while you stroke me,
ears to tail.
You'll soon find
you are growing sleepy.
When you wake up,
your headache will be gone.
Go ahead. Try it!"

Mrs. Weaver
slowly put out her hand
and began to move it
over George's fur.
She had never felt anything
so deliciously soft
in her life.
Back and forth,
back and forth went her hand,
and more and more
she began to feel drowsy.

He pat-patted his way
downstairs into the big kitchen.
He saw the sandwiches
wrapped and ready,
and then jumped up
in one of the chairs and waited.

When Milly and Tommy came in,
they were quarreling.

"You stop bossing me!"
Tommy shouted.
"Just because you're older
you can't tell me what to do."

"I can so!" Milly shouted back.
"And you'd better wait for me
the next time
the way Mother told you to.
If you don't I'll..."

She had gripped
a clump of Tommy's hair
when George spoke up
in his small but very clear voice.

"That's enough," he said.
"I'm really surprised at you both."

At last,
  as George
    had predicted,
      she
        fell
         asleep.

He sat on for a long while,
and then, when he felt
it must be nearly time
for the children to be back
for lunch,
he hopped to the floor very quietly.

Milly and Tommy saw him then
for the first time,
their eyes growing larger
and larger.
Then they looked at each other
as though to say,
Do you see and hear what I do?

George adjusted his glasses.

"Would you let
any other little girl
pull your brother's hair, Milly?"
he asked.

"N-no," she said,
"I wouldn't."

"And you, Tommy.
There's a good reason
why you should wait
to walk home with Milly,
isn't there?"

"Y-yes," Tommy admitted.

"I should say so.
Crossing streets nowadays
has to be a careful business.
Friend of mine got killed
last week
by not watching out.
Of course
a dog was chasing him.
Well,
I guess we have things settled,
then,
so run along and wash your hands.
Girls first," he added.

When the children were seated
at the table,
they kept looking
at their visitor
and then at each other
in a very puzzled way.

"Should have introduced myself,"
the guest said.
"Name is George.
George H. Rabbit.
H stands for Hare.
My grandfather
was a Belgian Hare.
Very handsome.
Long ears and all that.
It's why I wear glasses,"
he added.

"Not to help your eyes?"
Milly asked in surprise.

"Not a bit.
Eyes are fine.
But my grandfather wore them,
so I do, too.
Upon occasion.
Adds to my appearance, I think."

The children
looked at each other again
and then back to George.

"Would you care for some lunch?"
Milly asked politely.
"We never eat quite all
our sandwiches."

"Thank you," said George.
"Just a modicum, please.
That means *a little*.
Always learn new words
when you can.
A bit of sandwich
would be a pleasant change.
I usually eat only young *greens*."

Both children
said *Oh!* at once
in a very meaningful tone.
George seemed to stiffen.

"I explained about that
to your mother.
We won't bring it up again.
How did school go
this morning?"

Milly and Tommy both sighed.

"My arithmetic wasn't right."

"Neither was mine,"
said Tommy.

"Dear me!"
George scratched one ear delicately.
"When do you do your homework?"

"Well, it's like this,"
Milly explained.
"We can watch television
before dinner,
but after we eat
we have to do our chores,
then our homework,
and then go to bed.
It's all very boring."

"I don't know," said George.
"That seems reasonable to me,
as long as you can see television
before dinner.
Where do you do your studying?"

"Right here.
On the kitchen table.
We like it this way,
for we have room
to spread out our papers,"
Tommy said.

"Good!" George replied.
"Tonight I'll help you.
Arithmetic is my best subject.
My grandfather taught me.
He was a wonder with numbers.
O.K.?"

"You really mean it?"
Milly asked breathlessly.

"I've just said so,"
George answered.
He raised a paw to his head.
"Honor of a rabbit!"
he pronounced solemnly.

"Oh, that will be wonderful!
We'd better go now
and speak to Mother.
She told us
she mightn't be down to lunch."
Milly had risen from her chair.

"No," said George.
"She's asleep.
Don't disturb her.
She'll be down here
when you get back from school,
I know."

"Will you be here then, too?"
Tommy asked eagerly.

"I'm not sure
just what my plans
for the afternoon
will be,"
George said.
"But I'll keep my promise
for the evening.
Run along now."

The children had stopped
looking surprised.
They both waved good-by to him
as though to a dear friend.

George finished
his bit of sandwich and cookie
and then made a tour
of the kitchen and entryway.
He finally discovered
a cozy little spot in the latter,
behind the clothes dryer
and next to the broom closet.
Here, no one could see him.

"Location is perfect,"
George said to himself.
He hopped in,
settled his head upon his paws
and went fast asleep.

When Milly and Tommy
came back from school,
they rushed back
through the kitchen
calling, "George! George!
Where are you?
George!"

But George remained quiet
in his hiding place.
He heard them talking excitedly
to their mother,
and then at last
start out with her in the car
to meet their father's train.
It was Mr. Weaver
whom George was anxious about.
He hardly knew
whether to introduce himself,
or not.
Men were different.

When the station wagon
rolled again along the drive,
the family all came in
the back way.
Milly was talking excitedly.

"But Father, he was *here*.
Really, truly!
He ate lunch with us.
And he can *talk*.
He even uses big words."

"And he wears *glasses!*"
Tommy added.
"And his name's George!"

"Well! Well!" Mr. Weaver said.
"Now, isn't that interesting!"

"But Mother saw him, too.
Didn't you, Mother?"

George turned his head
in order to hear
her answer more clearly.

"I either saw him
or I *dreamed* him,"
Mrs. Weaver said.

"Oh, Father,
you don't believe us,"
Milly cried.

"You look just the way you did
the day we saw the fairy
in the apple tree!"

"Mother saw something, too.
She said so,"
Tommy put in earnestly.

And then George heard
their father laugh.
It was a nice laugh, very tender.
He couldn't be sure
but he had the feeling somehow
that Mr. Weaver
was kissing Mrs. Weaver.

"I know now," he was saying,
"why our children
can see fairies
and rabbits who wear glasses!
Well,
I'm going to take a little rest.
This was a hard day in the office.
And if George comes in,"
he called back,
still laughing,
but in a different way,
"tell him
I'll be pleased to see him."

"That settles it,"
George said grimly to himself.
"I don't intend to meet him.
Ever. So there!"

From Milly's description
at lunch
he could tell now
just what was happening.
The children
were watching television
while their mother
prepared the dinner.
Nice smells came from the stove,
but George would have traded
all the food
for some lettuce leaves
and carrot tops
if he had had the choice.

He could hear the voices
from the dining room
while dinner was in progress
and then the children
moving about at their chores.

Tommy, apparently,
cleared the table
and emptied
the kitchen wastebasket;
Milly wiped the dishes.
When all was finished,
Mrs. Weaver spoke.

"Now children,
start your homework.
And please try hard
to do it properly.
I hope
your next month's report cards
will be better than the last time.
I'm going into the living room now
with Father,
and you can watch the clock,
Tommy.
At eight sharp,
you must be off to bed.
Then Milly at eight-thirty."

George came out of his nook
very softly,
for he didn't want anyone
to know his hiding place.

As he entered the kitchen
Milly was saying,
almost in tears,
"But he *promised!*"

"And here I am,"
said George briskly,
jumping up on a chair
between them.
"Now, let's begin.
What do you have to do, Tommy?"

The children
were so happy to see him
that for a few moments
they couldn't speak.
They just stroked his soft back,
turn about,
and Milly
even placed a little kiss
between his ears.
He shook his head a bit after this,
for he wasn't sure
he liked being kissed.
The stroking was all right.
And of course
he was happy
that the children
were fond of him.

"Well, Tommy?" he repeated.

"I have to have
the *four times* table perfect.
I missed it today."

"And I have
some dreadful examples
in addition and subtraction both!
I'll never get them right!"
Milly groaned.

"Of course you will.
Just buckle down to it.
Concentrate.
That means
make your mind work hard.
I'll hear Tommy's table
while you do your problems."

Tommy always made a mistake
when he got to four times nine.
Each time he said *thirty-four.*
George puckered up his eyes
as though thinking.

"I'll tell you!" he said.
"The right answer
rhymes with *sticks.*
Now, you remember that
and try it again.
From the beginning."

Tommy repeated slowly
and finally said,
"Four times nine is —
sticks — *thirty-six!*"

"Fine!" said George.
"Now say it all over twice,
and I think you'll have it!"

When Tommy was through
and very pleased, indeed,
with himself,
George turned to Milly's paper
and scanned it carefully.

"It is my considered opinion,"
he said at last,
"that according to
my grandfather's teaching,
these problems are all right!"

Milly clapped her hands.
"If I get a hundred on this
tomorrow,
I'll be so happy!
You know, George,
I really worked hard tonight.
Usually I keep getting up
to call one of my friends
on the phone
or look at the clock
or chatter to Tommy.
It's so much easier
when you are beside us.
Will you be here each night?"

"For a while," said George.
"I like it here.
Nice house.
Nice family.
Eight o'clock, Tommy.
You'd better scamper."

"Couldn't you come up,
when we're in bed?
Please, George!"
Tommy was almost breathless,
he was so eager.

"Well, well, hurry along.
We'll see."

Tommy didn't argue
or complain
or delay
as he usually did.
He put up his book,
said goodnight to his father
and fairly ran up the stairs.
Later
when Milly was in the living room
and Mrs. Weaver
had heard Tommy's prayers,
kissed him
and come back down again,
George quietly pat-patted up.
He heard Tommy's low *hoo-hoo*
so he knew which room
to go into.
Once there
he jumped on the bed
and snuggled close to Tommy.
The little boy
put his arms around his new friend
and drew a long breath.

"You're so soft
. . . and comfortable, George.
I really love you!"
And in a very few minutes
he was fast asleep.

George waited a while,
then got down
and sat under the bed.
He heard Milly come up
and move around in the next room.
He heard Mrs. Weaver come later
and say goodnight,
then all was quiet.
He hopped into Milly's room
and leaped up beside her.
Milly drew him close to her
and kissed him again
between his ears.
He didn't mind so much this time.
In fact he rather liked it.

"Please stay on with us, George,"
she begged.
"It's so wonderful
having a rabbit like you
in the family."

She stroked his fur gently
for a little while
and then she, too, fell asleep.

As George was going downstairs,
he overheard
the children's parents
talking in the living room.

"It was amazing,"
Mrs. Weaver said,
"how quickly
Tommy and Milly
went to bed tonight!
I've been having a lot of trouble
with them lately.
They keep fussing
and wanting drinks of water
and all sorts of things."

"Oh, it's just a phase
they've been going through,"
Mr. Weaver said very wisely,
"and they've gotten over it now.
Besides,
they probably were tired tonight."

George snickered to himself.
"A lot he knows about it!"
he thought.

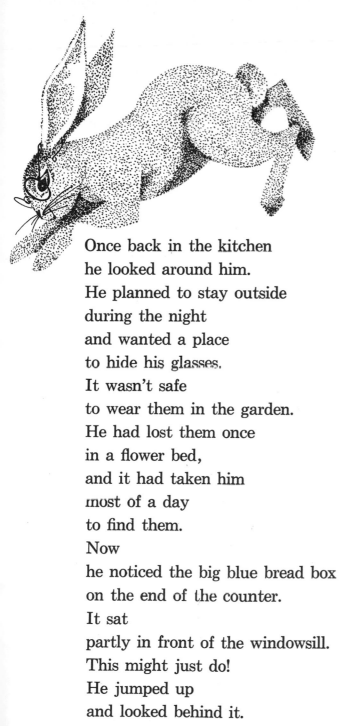

Once back in the kitchen
he looked around him.
He planned to stay outside
during the night
and wanted a place
to hide his glasses.
It wasn't safe
to wear them in the garden.
He had lost them once
in a flower bed,
and it had taken him
most of a day
to find them.
Now
he noticed the big blue bread box
on the end of the counter.
It sat
partly in front of the windowsill.
This might just do!
He jumped up
and looked behind it.

Anything on the sill
back of the box
would be completely hidden.
George carefully took off
his glasses,
folded them
and laid them on the sill.
Then he got down
and went to the back screen door.
He knew it didn't fasten well,
for Tommy
was always leaving it unlatched.
He scratched now with one paw,
then nudged it with his nose.
At last it opened,
and he hopped out
into the lovely, soft spring darkness.

using your ears in reading

You boys and girls
went into a movie
one Saturday afternoon
and came out with this word
ringing in your ears:

Supercalifragilisticexpialidocious.

From that moment forward,
you've had no difficulty
singing and reading the word.
The question is,
when you're reading this word now,
are you reading it with your eyes
or with your ears?
Consider another example
of how our ears tell our eyes
what they are seeing:

One-amy, uery, hickory, seven,
    Hallibone, crackable,
       ten and eleven,
Peep-O, it must be done,
Twiggle, twaggle, twenty-one.

If you happen to have heard
this old counting rhyme before,
you probably will have
no trouble reading it
with the right rhythm
and pronunciation;
but if you haven't heard it before,
you surely have a struggle in store.

This shows that it's not easy
to read some sentences
if you've never heard their sound.
It might be fun to see
how long it takes you
    and your class
to learn how to read this rhyme.
You'll discover
that you read it better
as you become more familiar
with its sound.

Now, look at the words
    done and *one*
that appear in the rhyme.
These are words
that you learned "in the ear."
No phonic rules can tell you
how to pronounce them.

                An essay by Bill Martin, Jr.

And if you want further proof
of our reliance on our ear
   in reading,
just consider this list of words:
   done   one   ton   sun   won.
Then there are other complications
when you add such words as
   tone   on   gone.

Learning to read
even certain simple words
in our language
depends on good ear training.

A good reader learns to hear
what he is reading
even when he is reading to himself.
Certain printed language symbols,
like a question mark
and an exclamation point
and a period,
remind him of the sound
of the sentences.
For example,
a story may tell of a mother
fixing breakfast cereal
for her son.
She asks, *"With milk?"*
He answers, *"With milk."*

Although the words are the same,
they don't sound the same
to the reader.
He hears the mother's voice go up,
and he hears the son's voice
   go down,
because his ears are helping him
get the meaning
from the printed page.

Now look at the following poem.
It may seem strange
until you hear it read aloud.
If you want to test the importance
of the ear in reading,
divide your class in half.
One part
will read the poem silently
several times.
The other half
will listen to your teacher
read it aloud several times
while following the reading
in your own books.
Then come together,
and have each group
read the poem aloud.
Which group
has the easiest time reading it?

Five Little Bats

Five little bats flew out of the attic:
Five little bats all acrobatic

One little bat flew through the city,
One little bat was flitting pretty.

One little bat flew round the gable,
One little bat was not flight able.

One little bat flew in and out of
Something or other, I haven't a doubt of

That, or that five little bats erratic
Flew back in and are now up attic.

A poem by David McCord

The next time you need help
in reading something complicated,
why not ask your best friend
or your teacher
to read it aloud for you?

This is not a lazy way
of learning to read.
It is the most sensible way
of putting your ears in tune
with the printed page.

On the following three pages
(and elsewhere
throughout the book)
are selections that will help you
use your ears to guide your eyes
through a sentence.

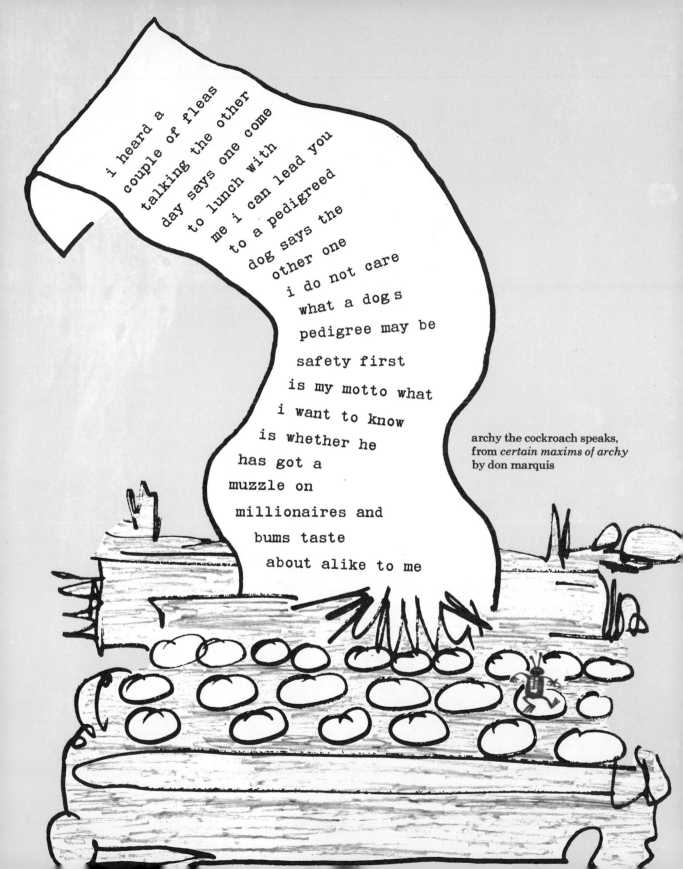

i heard a
couple of fleas
talking the other
day says one come
to lunch with
me i can lead you
to a pedigreed
dog says the
other one
i do not care
what a dogs
pedigree may be
safety first
is my motto what
i want to know
is whether he
has got a
muzzle on
millionaires and
bums taste
about alike to me

archy the cockroach speaks,
from *certain maxims of archy*
by don marquis

The Sea Wolf

Here is a poem that will fill the mind with haunting pictures of fishermen riding out the fury of storms at sea. As you read it aloud together, let your voices show the rising and the passing of the storm.

The fishermen say, when your catch is done
And you're sculling in with the tide,
You must take great care that the Sea Wolf's share
Is tossed to him overside.

They say that the Sea Wolf rides by day,
Unseen on the crested waves,
And the sea mists rise from his cold green eyes
When he comes from his salt sea caves.

The fishermen say, when it storms at night
And the great seas bellow and roar,
That the Sea Wolf rides on the plunging tides,
And you hear his howl at the door.

And you must throw open your door at once,
And fling your catch to the waves,
Till he drags his share to his cold sea lair,
Straight down to his salt sea caves.

Then the storm will pass, and the still stars shine,
In peace — so the fishermen say —
But the Sea Wolf waits by the cold Sea Gates
For the dawn of another day.

A poem by Violet McDougal,
    picture by Terri Payor

EVERYBODY

LOVES

SATURDAY NIGHT

EVERYBODY

EVERYBODY

EVERYBODY

EVERYBODY

EVERYBODY

LOVES

SATURDAY NIGHT

This joyful Nigerian folk song has no particular message. As you read it aloud, your ears begin to tell you that it is a happy, bouncy ditty. Your ears also will begin telling you that the words loves *and* night *are either drawn out or are followed by a pause as you speak them, to preserve the rhythm.*

Because everyone everywhere seems to enjoy Saturday night, we have printed the first line of the song in many languages. Can you figure out which word (or words) in each language is Saturday, night, and everybody? And if you can do that, you certainly can figure out the word loves. But isn't it interesting, until you have heard each language spoken, you have no notion of how to read these lines aloud.... Yes, language truly is learned in the ear!

French:	Tout le monde aime Samedi soir.
Yiddish:	Jeder eyne hot lieb Shabas ba nacht.
Russian:	Vsiem nravitsa Sabota vietcheram.
Ukrainian:	Kozhdi lubit Subotu vechir.
Czech:	Kazhdi ma rad Sabotu vietcher.
Polish:	Kazdy lubi Soboty wieczur.
German:	Jedermann liebt Samstag Abend.
Spanish:	Todo el mundo le gusta la noche del Sábado.
Japanese:	Dare demo doyobi ga suki.
Chinese:	Ren ren shi huan li pei lu.
Hebrew:	Kol echad ohev Shabat ba laila.
Hawaiian:	Ke puni kela mea i Po'aono po.

maggie and milly and molly and may
went down to the beach (to play one day)

and maggie discovered a shell that sang
so sweetly she couldn't remember her troubles, and

milly befriended a stranded star
whose rays five languid fingers were;

and molly was chased by a horrible thing
which raced sideways while blowing bubbles: and

may came home with a smooth round stone
as small as a world and as large as alone.

For whatever we lose (like a you or a me)
it's always ourselves we find in the sea

a poem by e. e. cummings

here's a poem without capital letters.
that's how the poet wrote it and that's
how we're printing it. isn't it intriguing?
we have also omitted the title so that
you can have fun making up your own.

Full of the Moon

A poem by Karla Kuskin,
picture by Frank Aloise

It's full of the moon,
The dogs dance out
Through brush and bush and bramble.
They howl and yowl
And growl and prowl.
They amble, ramble, scramble.
They rush through brush.
They push through bush.
They yip and yap and hurr.
They lark around and bark around
With prickles in their fur.
They two-step in the meadow.
They polka on the lawn.
Tonight's the night
The dogs dance out
And chase their tails till dawn.

As you read this poem, your ears tell you
to read it in a frolicking way.
They also tell you that
the author is having fun with words
and is inviting you to do the same.

An essay by Bill Martin, Jr.

using your eyes to hear

It's no news to you
that you use your eyes
when you read the printed page.
Your eyes pick up
all kinds of signals,
such as

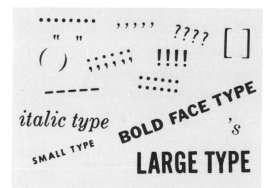

You know these signals already.
You use them when you write.
You also use them
when you read
what someone else has written.

In this book, you are invited
to use your eyes in many ways
that trigger your voice
to respond to print.
Look at "Giant Thunder," page 64.
How does the type
give you the mood of the poem?
How does that influence
your reading of the poem?
Now look at "Shinny Bone," page 16.
What sounds do you find
in the type?
Now look at page 50.
The signals on this page
tell a story without words.
That is why you don't
just look at pictures—
you read them.

And now let's have some fun
with eye-sound signals.
David McCord's poem,
"At the Garden Gate,"
is laden with sound signals
because he wants you
to read the poem
in the same way
that he hears it.
Can you find the sound signals
in the poem?
Can you follow them
as you read the poem aloud?

AT THE GARDEN GATE

Who so late
at the garden gate?
Emily, Kate,
and John.
"*John*
where have you been?
It's after six
Supper is on,
And you've been gone
An hour,
John!"
"We've been, we've been,
We've just been over
The field," said
John.
(Emily, Kate,
and John.)

Who so late
at the garden gate?
Emily, Kate,
and John.
"John,
what have you got?"
"A whopping toad.
Isn't he big?
He's a terrible
Load.
(We found him
A little ways
Up the road,"
said Emily,
Kate,
and John.)

Who so late
at the garden gate?
Emily, Kate,
and John.
"*John,*
put that thing down!
Do you want to get warts?"
(They all three have 'em
By last
Reports.)
Still, finding toads
Is the best of
Sports,
Say Emily,
Kate,
and John.

A poem by David McCord

A Picture for Storytelling

Picture by Michael Lowenbein

 the Duel

This classic poem has been beloved by boys and girls for generations, and by adults who remember that clocks can talk and plates can turn blue with fright. Begin by reading it in unison. Then do it in parts as a choral reading, slowly, as a mysterious and awesome event.

The gingham dog and the calico cat
Side by side on the table sat:
'T was half-past twelve, and (what do you think!)
Nor one nor t' other had slept a wink!
　　The old Dutch clock and the Chinese plate
　　Appeared to know as sure as fate
There was going to be a terrible spat.
　　(I wasn't there; I simply state
　　What was told to me by the Chinese plate!)

The gingham dog went, "Bow-wow-wow!"
And the calico cat replied, "Mee-ow!"
The air was littered, an hour or so,
With bits of gingham and calico,
　　While the old Dutch clock in the chimney-place
　　Up with its hands before its face,
For it always dreaded a family row!
　　(Now mind: I'm only telling you
　　What the old Dutch clock declares is true!)

The Chinese plate looked very blue,
And wailed, "Oh, dear! what shall we do!"
But the gingham dog and the calico cat
Wallowed this way and tumbled that,
　　Employing every tooth and claw
　　In the awfullest way you ever saw—
And, oh! how the gingham and calico flew!
　　(Don't fancy I exaggerate—
　　I got my news from the Chinese plate!)

Next morning, where the two had sat,
They found no trace of dog or cat;
And some folks think unto this day
That burglars stole that pair away!
　　But the truth about the cat and pup
　　Is this: they ate each other up!
Now what do you really think of that!
　　(The old Dutch clock, it told me so,
　　And that is how I came to know.)

A poem by Eugene Field
with pictures by Albert John Pucci

KEMO KIMO

	1	2	3	4
In	Car -	o -	li - na	the
	folks	all	go,	☐
	Sing	song	kitty,	can't you
	ki -	me -	oh?	☐
	There's	where the	folks	all
	plant	the	tow.	☐
	Sing	song	kitty,	can't you
	ki -	me -	oh?	☐
	Cover	the	ground	all
	over	with	smoke,	☐
	Sing	song	kitty,	can't you
	ki -	me -	oh?	☐
	Then	their	heads	a -
	round	they	poke.	☐
	Sing	song	kitty,	can't you
	ki -	me -	oh?	☐
	Ke -	mo	ki -	mo,
	there,	oh	where?	With my
	hi,	my	ho,	and
	in	comes	Sally,	singin'
	Some -	time	penny -	winkle
	ling -	tum	nip -	cat,
	Sing	song	kitty,	can't you
	ki -	me -	oh?	☐

In Carolina the folks all go,

Sing song kitty, can't you ki-me-oh?

There's where the folks all plant the tow.

Sing song kitty, can't you ki-me-oh?

Cover the ground all over with smoke,

Sing song kitty, can't you ki-me-oh?

Then their heads around they poke.

Sing song kitty, can't you ki-me-oh?

      Ke-mo ki-mo, there, oh where?

With my hi, my ho, and in comes Sally, singin'

Sometime penny-winkle ling-tum nip-cat,

Sing song kitty, can't you ki-me-oh?

There was a frog lived in a pool,

Sing song kitty, can't you ki-me-oh?

Sure he was the biggest fool.

Sing song kitty, can't you ki-me-oh?

He could dance and he could sing.

Sing song kitty, can't you ki-me-oh?

Make the woods around him ring.

Sing song kitty, can't you ki-me-oh?

      Ke-mo ki-mo, there, oh where?

With my hi, my ho, and in comes Sally, singin'

Sometime penny-winkle ling-tum nip-cat,

Sing song kitty, can't you ki-me-oh?

This lively song from the Kentucky mountains is sheer nonsense,
but its rhythm and use of strange words
have made it a favorite with people everywhere.
The first verse of the song has been set up
to help you fit the syllables of words to the 1-2-3-4 beat of the rhythm.
Isn't it interesting to see how the words are syllabicated to fit the rhythm?
The words should be chanted or sung
(to your own tune, if you don't know the original melody).

A folktale adapted by Bill Martin, Jr.   Woodcuts by Susan Blair

The Gunny Wolf

A man and his little daughter lived alone in a forest—
oh, how he loved her—
and there were wolves in the forest.
So the man built a fence round the house
and told his little daughter,
"You must on no account go outside the gate
while I am away."

One morning when he had gone away,
the little girl was hunting for flowers
and thought it would do no harm
just to peep through the gate.
So she did.
She saw a little flower so near
that she stepped outside to pick it.
Then she saw another a little farther off
and went for that.
Then she saw another and went for that,

and so she kept getting
farther and farther
away from home.

As she picked the flowers,
she sang a little song,
   *"Tray-blah,
   tray-blah,
   cum-qua,
   ki-mo."*

(This is sung
in a childish voice.)

Suddenly she heard a noise
and looked up
and saw a great gunny wolf,
and he said,

(This is said
in a low, gruff voice.)

"Sing that sweeten,
gooden song again."

(Childish voice)

She sang,
"*Tray-blah,*
tray-blah,
cum-qua,
ki-mo."

Wolf, he gone.

(This is said softly and quickly
to represent the child's footsteps.)

Pit-a-pat, pit-a-pat,
pit-a-pat, pit-a-pat.
She goes back.

(This is said rapidly
in a coarse, deep voice.)

Presently she hears
pit-a-pat, pit-a-pat,
pit-a-pat, pit-a-pat
coming behind her,
and there was the wolf,
an' 'e says,

(Gruff voice)

"You move?"

(Childish voice)

"Oh no, my dear.
What 'casion I move?"

Wolf: "Sing that sweeten
            gooden song again."

            She sang,
Child: *"Tray-blah,*
              tray-blah,
              cum-qua,
              ki-mo."

            Wolf, he gone.

(Delicately)   *Pit-a-pat, pit-a-pat,*
               pit-a-pat, pit-a-pat.
            She goes back some more.

	Presently she hears
(Coarsely)	*pit-a-pat, pit-a-pat,*
	pit-a-pat, pit-a-pat
	coming behind her,
	and there was the wolf,
	an' 'e says,
Wolf:	"You move!"

| Child: | "Oh no, my dear.
What 'casion I move?" |

| Wolf: | "Sing that sweeten,
gooden song again." |

	She sang,
Child:	*"Tray,*
	blah-tray,
	blah-cum
	qua-ki-mo."

Wolf, he gone.

| (Delicately) | *Pit-a-pat, pit-a-pat.*
She goes back some more. |

	Presently she hears
(Coarsely)	*pit-a-pat, pit-a-pat*
	coming behind her,
	and there was the wolf,
	an' 'e says,
Wolf:	"YOU MOVE!"

Child: "Oh no, my dear.
What 'casion I move?"

Wolf: "Sing that sweeten,
gooden song again."

Child: She sang,
*"Tray-blah-tray,
blah-cum-qua,
ki-mo."*

Wolf, he gone.

(Delicately) *Pit-a-pat, pit-a-pat, pit-a-pat,
pit-a-pat, pit-a-pat, pit-a-pat.*
She goes back some more,

and this time when she hears
(Coarsely) *pit-a-pat, pit-a-pat, pit-a-pat,
pit-a-pat, pit-a-pat, pit-a-pat*
coming behind her,
she slips inside the gate
and SHUTS it,
(Read the word *shuts*
like the sound
of a gate slamming.) and wolf,
he can't get her.

HippyHippoThe

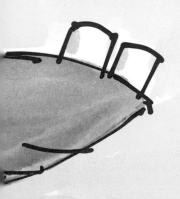

UN
HappyHippopotamus

A story by William D. Sheldon,
pictures by Ed Renfro

Hippy Hippo, the (un) happy hippopotamus, was hungry.
For days he had grown hungrier and hungrier.
Today he felt that he could stand it no longer.
So he opened his mouth and let out a loud cry.

OOOWWWWW!

The monkeys *chattered*,   the snakes *hissed*,

the wolves *howled*,   the bears *growled*,

and   the lions *roared*.

They, *too*, were hungry.

Freddy,
the Friendly Animal Keeper,
stood outside Hippy's cage.
"I am sorry," he said.
"I know you are hungry.
All the animals are hungry.
I am hungry, too.
There is no more money
to buy goods.
The circus is *broke!*"

Hippy could not understand
what Freddy,
the Friendly Keeper, said.
All he knew was
that Freddy shoveled less
and less food
into his cage each day.

Hippy was sad.
"If I don't have
a full meal soon,
I will shrink to a shadow."

It was true, of course.
Hippy had become thin.
He weighed less
than 6000 pounds.
He would soon be
a very thin hippopotamus.

Hippy Is Sold at Auction

A great many excited people
gathered around the animal tent
waiting for the auction to begin.
Alice Brown and her friends
were fascinated by Hippy.
They stood around his cage,
unable to take their eyes off him.

"Look at him," said Alice.
"What a sad, sad hippopotamus."
"Yes," said one of her friends,
"he looks awfully sad."

Freddy, the Friendly Keeper,
said,
"Yes, Hippy Hippo is
a very sad hippopotamus.
He is very hungry.
Each day I used to feed him
   100 pounds of grass,
   200 pounds of hay,
    50 pounds of water plants,
    50 pounds of rice plants,
and
   many many tender tree shoots."

Freddy looked sadder and sadder
as he spoke.
"Then, when we began
to run out of money,
I had to cut down on his food.
Yesterday I only fed Hippy
 50 pounds of grass,
 100 pounds of hay,
 25 pounds of water plants,
 25 pounds of rice plants,
and
 no tender tree shoots.
No wonder he is
such a sad hippopotamus."

Hippy watched the girls
as they walked with Freddy
and joined the crowd of people.
A man suddenly began
shouting out to the people.
He was the auctioneer
who had come to sell
the animals of the circus.
"What am I bid
for this beautiful golden lion?"
he shouted.
"Let's hear it. What am I bid?"

Hippy couldn't understand
what was happening.
He just stood
and grew hungrier and hungrier

The people bid on the animals.
Finally, the auctioneer pointed
to Hippy.
"Here," he said, "is one
of the finest hippopotamuses
in the world.
He is happy
and contented and loves people.
Now who will be the first
to bid for Hippy Hippo?"

Suddenly,
Alice Brown cried out,
"I will! I bid $400.00!"

"$400.00!"
exclaimed the auctioneer.
"Where did a little girl like you
get $400.00?"

"I have it," said Alice,
pulling the money
out of her dress pocket.

There was silence all around.
No one said a word.
The auctioneer shouted,
"Going, going, going, gone
for $400.00
to the young lady
in the brown hat.
You are a lucky young lady.
This is a *great* hippopotamus."

The girls shouted and ran
over to Hippy Hippo's cage.
Freddy joined them.
"What are you going to do
with Hippy?" he asked.
"How are you going to feed him?
Where are you
going to keep him?"

Alice and her friends
stared at Hippy.
"I know," said Alice,
"I will call my father.
He'll know what to do."
Alice went to a phone booth
and called her father.

"Hello, Daddy," she cried.
"I just bought a hippopotamus."

"A *what?*" shouted her father.
"You *bought* a what?"

"A hippopotamus!"
Alice cried again.
"But I don't know
what to do with him."

"*Where* are you?"
shouted Mr. Brown.

"At the circus grounds
in Munnsville," Alice replied.

"Wait for me there,"
said her father.
"*Don't move* until I get there!"

Hippy Goes Home

When Alice's father arrived,
he looked at Hippy Hippo.
Then *he looked* at Alice.

"All right," he said.
"We'll haul him home in his cage.
Then we will *decide*
what to do with him."

Alice and her friends
helped Mr. Brown and Freddy
fasten Hippy's cage to the car.
They all said good-by to Freddy
and drove home.

As they drove along,
the girls turned around
and watched Hippy.
All of a sudden,
he opened his mouth
and made a big noise.
He sounded bad.
"Owwwwwww! Owwwwwww!"

"Owwwwwww!" he groaned.
"Owwwwwww!"

Mr. Brown stopped the car,
and everyone got out.
"What is the matter with him?"
said Mr. Brown.

"He is probably hungry,"
said Alice.

"Well," said Mr. Brown,
"did anyone tell you
what we should feed him?"

"Yes," said Alice timidly.
"Yes, Freddy told us. He needs
    100 pounds of grass,
    200 pounds of hay,
     50 pounds of water plants,
     50 pounds of rice plants,
and, *if possible,*
    some tender tree shoots."

"*What!*" shouted Mr. Brown.
"Where are we going
to get *all that food?*
This is terrible.
How am I going to buy
all that food for Hippy?"

Hippy didn't understand
what the people were saying.
All he knew was
that he was hungry.

"Come on," cried Mr. Brown.
"Let's find him something to eat."

They all got back into the car
and drove and drove.
Hippy groaned and groaned.
Finally they reached
a big roadside stand.
Mr. Brown got out
and talked to the owner
of the stand.
Soon, everyone was carrying
food to Hippy.
They gave him
    some grass,
    some hay,
    some water plants,
    a little rice plant,
but
    no tender tree shoots.

Hippy ate and ate and ate,
and finally he ate no more —
the food was all gone.

Mr. Brown paid the owner
of the food stand
and got into the car.

171

As he drove, he kept thinking
how much it was going to cost
to feed Hippy —
more than his entire family.
What was he going to do?

They finally arrived
in Mr. Brown's home town.
Mr. Brown drove
to his home slowly.
People stared and stared.
Some boys and girls,
men and women,
and even a few dogs followed
Mr. Brown and Hippy Hippo.

Mr. Brown finally
reached his home
and got out of his car.
By that time, the cage
was surrounded with people
all shouting and looking at Hippy.

The Town Feeds Hippy

Mr. Brown waved his hands
to make the people stop shouting.
"My daughter bought Hippy Hippo
from the circus in Munnsville,"
he said. "I do not know
what we are going to do with him.
He is hungry
and if I feed him every day,

I will *not* be able
to feed my family. He eats
    too much grass,
    too much hay,
    too many water plants,
    too many rice plants,
and sometimes
    too many tender tree shoots
EVERY DAY."

One man spoke up:
"I have some hay."
Then another said,
"I can give him grass."
Soon all the people left to get food,
and Mr. Brown
dragged Hippy's cage
into the backyard of his home.

In a little while,
boys and girls,
and men and women,
began to return
to the Browns' home.
They all carried something
for Hippy to eat. They gave him
    a great deal of grass,
    some hay,
    very few water plants,
    hardly any rice plants,
and
    no tender tree shoots.

An Ad in the Paper

Mr. and Mrs. Brown and Alice
sat down that evening.

Mr. Brown looked very worried.
"What can we do?" he said.
"Our friends can't feed Hippy
and we can't either."

"We have to sell Hippy,"
Alice said. "I know.
We can put an ad in the paper.
It can read:

FOR SALE: Hippopotamus, happy,
$400.00. EX. 9-6520."

"That's a good idea,"
said Mr. Brown.
"We'll do it right away."

The Browns waited
for someone to answer the ad.
For three days they waited,
but no one called.
Hippy ate and ate.
Mr. Brown's friends were tired
of bringing food,
and the Browns were running out
of money.

Mr. and Mrs. Brown and Alice
sat down again.
"I know," said Mr. Brown.
"We'll lower the price to $200.00."

And they did.

But no one answered the ad,
and Hippy ate and ate and ate.
Now all the friends came
and said they could not bring
any more food.
The man at the bank called
and told Mr. Brown
that his checking account
was very low.

"I am going to put another ad
in the paper," Mr. Brown said.
"It will say:

PERSONAL: Happy Hippo needs a new home.
Will deliver him free of charge."

The next day
the Browns' telephone rang.
Mr. Brown *ran* to answer it.
"Can I help you?" he asked.

"Do you own a hippo
that you want to give away?"
said the voice on the phone.

Mr. Brown sighed with relief.
"Yes, we do," he said.
"*Free of charge!*"

"I am the City Zoo Keeper,"
replied the voice.
"We need a hippopotamus
and will come and get him."

Hippy Happy at the Zoo

Hippy was now in the zoo.
Each day a friendly Zoo Keeper
shoveled into his cage

100 *pounds* of grass,
200 *pounds* of hay,
50 *pounds* of water plants,
50 *pounds* of rice plants,
and always
many many tender tree shoots.

Hippy ate and ate and ate.
He grew larger and larger
and larger.

Alice and her father went
to the zoo and watched Hippy eat.
"He looks happy," said Mr. Brown.

"Yes," said Alice.
"*My* Hippy Hippo.
I am so glad he is happy."

Hippy rolled his eyes
up at Alice,
shook his head,
and ate and ate and ate.

174

Have you ever started
reading a story
and suddenly had a hunch
that you knew
how it would turn out?
Of course, you have.
Everyone has.
A hunch of this kind
is a real help in reading.

using literary

STRUCTURE

TO SIMPLIFY READING

Every good reader I've known
has these hunches and uses them
to get more enjoyment and meaning
from the printed page.
Sometimes his hunches even
help him read words
that he has never seen before.
In this dialogue,
you and I are going to explore
some of these hunches
and how they can be used.

Everything you read
has been put together
according to the author's plan.
Once you discover this plan,
you begin to see
how the author is thinking.
When you know his pattern,
then you can move out
ahead of the author
and predict
what is going to follow.
It makes no difference
whether your predictions always
follow the author's thinking.
The fact that you predicted
makes you a more interested reader—
and, therefore, a better
and more appreciative reader.

Now for some practice.

1

Consider how the structure
of the following story
helps you know
what is coming next.
It is the first part
of "The Three Little Pigs
and the Ogre,"
found on page 185 in this book.

"Aha!" says the great wicked ogre, "it is a nice plump little pig that I have been wanting for my supper this many a day past. So you may just come along with me now."

"Oh, Master Ogre," squeaked the smallest of the little pigs in the smallest of voices — "oh, Master Ogre, don't eat me! There is a bigger pig back of me, and he will be along presently."

So the ogre let the smallest of the little pigs go, for he would rather have a larger pig if he could get it.

Knowing just this much
of the story,
you can guess
much of the language
that will be used in the story
when the ogre meets
the second little pig
and, finally,
the third little pig.

You've already guessed
that the parts
of the conversation above,
printed in blue,
are likely to be repeated
when the second little pig
meets the ogre.
(This will be
the second episode of the story.)

And you may be saying,
"Aha! this is one
of those repetitive stories,
so I already know
how it is put together."
(In a repetitive story,
each episode
tends to repeat an earlier one.)
You also may be thinking
that the third little pig
(third episode)
will outwit the ogre
with a different plan
from the ones used
by the first two little pigs.
Therefore, his conversation
with the ogre
will be somewhat different
from theirs.

Now, let's think
of the story itself.
What is the story problem.
The ogre wants to eat
the pigs,
and the pigs must find
a way to escape.
Every story is built
around a problem.
The solving of that problem
is what makes up the story.
Once you sense
the story problem,
you find yourself wide awake
to the first hint of a way
that the problem
is going to be solved.
Using hunches like this
in reading helps you
to read along swiftly,
with understanding
and increasing pleasure.

2

Sometimes when you look at a page,
the picture and type design
give you a hunch
of what kind of a story
you'll be reading.
This is what the artists
in magazines and books
often try to do—
make the pictures and type designs
give you a clue
about the mood of the article.
The design on the next page
will tell you immediately
that you'll be reading
something amusing,
something zany.
It's an old song
that I learned in my childhood
and have never forgotten.
I hope you don't get dizzy
as you go round and round.

The Music Goes 'Round and Around

Lyrics by "Red" Hodgson,
illustration by Frank Aloise

3

Sometimes you get a hunch
very early in the story
about its outcome,
and when you finish reading,
you say to yourself,
"I knew it would turn out
that way."
Good readers are alert
to the clues in a story
that help them make reasonable
hunches about what will happen.
Farther back in this book
is the story "Rikki-tikki-tavi."
The clues that appear
in the first six sentences
pretty much spell out
what is going to happen
in the story.
Let's turn to pages 258 and 259
to look at those sentences
and discover what notions
they give you about the story.
(Now turn to pages 258 and 259
and read those six sentences.
I'll wait here until you return.)

Do you agree
that the clues in these sentences
point to a terrible battle
between Rikki-tikki-tavi
and the snakes?
Was there any clue
that Teddy and his family
would be part of that battle?
The father said that the mongoose
would be a *protection*.
For whom?
The mother was worried.
What does this forecast
about the mood of the story?
Is it going to be
a humorous story
or a serious story?
How will the story turn out?
Hunches like these,
pleasantly enough,
do not rob the story
of its excitement.
They always stay as hunches
until the story proves
or disproves them.

4

When you have a hunch
about the story,
it's not like having someone
tell you the story.
You never can be exactly sure
about hunches, except that
they make you a better reader.
Did you ever start reading a poem
and suddenly have a hunch
that you knew the next line?
Well, try guessing the last line
of this jingle:

I'll tell you a story
About Jack a Nory,
And now my story's begun;
I'll tell you another
About Jack and his brother,
. . . .

Now, what's the last line?
You have a strong clue
in the structure of this jingle.
Notice that the thought
and structure of lines 1 and 2
are echoed in lines 4 and 5.
You, therefore, can reason
in a similar way that the last line
will echo the thought and structure
of the third line.
Right?

You also can make a hunch
that the third and last lines
will rhyme.
Yes, the last line is,
"And now my story is done."
Isn't it interesting
that if you had never seen
the word *done* before,
even though you knew
all the phonic rules,
you would have no notion
of its correct pronunciation.
But the kind of help you get
from the structure of this jingle
tells you exactly
how to pronounce this word.

And now, let's have
a little fun with hunches.
How long will it take you
to catch onto the mood
and structure
of this jingle,
even to reading words
that aren't there?

　　　　　　　　An essay by Bill Martin, Jr.

I came to the river...

I came to the river and I couldn't get across,

I jumped on a frog 'cause I thought he was a hoss,

The hoss wouldn't pull so I traded for a bull,

The bull wouldn't holler so I sold him for a dollar,

The dollar wouldn't pass so I threw it in the grass,

The grass wouldn't grow so I traded for a hoe,

The hoe wouldn't dig so I traded for a pig,

--- --- --------- squeal -- - ------ --- - wheel,

--- ----- --------- run -- - ------ --- - gun,

--- --- --------- shoot -- - ------ --- - boot,

--- ---- -------- fit -- - thought I'd quit,

And I did.

American folklore

A Busy City

A busy city
is like a beehive.
It sweeps people along
in many different directions,
causing each of them
to feel and to see
widely different things.
In this painting,
a young painter named
Lourdes Armas de Antillano
gives us a glimpse
of what he feels and sees
in the city of Maracaibo,
built on the edge of a lake
in Venezuela, South America.
What kind of feelings
and sights
does your home town
stir in you?
Why not express them
in a painting or poem
or story or song
or dance or play?

My Favorite Things

A song by Richard Rodgers and Oscar Hammerstein II,
picture by Betty Fraser

Raindrops on roses and whiskers on kittens,
Bright copper kettles and warm woolen mittens,
Brown paper packages tied up with strings,
These are a few of my favorite things.

Cream-colored ponies and crisp apple strudels,
Doorbells and sleighbells and schnitzel with noodles,
Wild geese that fly with the moon on their wings,
These are a few of my favorite things.

Girls in white dresses with blue satin sashes,
Snowflakes that stay on my nose and eyelashes,
Silver-white winters that melt into springs,
These are a few of my favorite things.

When the dog bites,
When the bee stings,
When I'm feeling sad,
I simply remember my favorite things
And then I don't feel so bad.

Story and pictures by Howard P. Pyle

The Three Little Pigs
and the
OGRE

HERE were three nice, fat little pigs. The first was small, the second was smaller, and the third was the smallest of all. And these three little pigs thought of going out into the woods to gather acorns.

"There's a great ogre who lives over yonder in the woods," says the barnyard cock.

Sensing the story problem

"And he will eat you up, body and bones," says the speckled hen.

"And there will be an end of you," says the black drake.

"If folks only knew what was good for them, they would stay at home and make the best of what they had there," says the old gray goose who laid eggs under the barn and who had never gone out into the world or had had a peep of it beyond the garden gate.

But no; the little pigs would go out into the world, whether or no. So out into the woods they went.

The story problem

They hunted for acorns here and they hunted for acorns there, and by and by whom should the smallest of all the little pigs meet but the great, wicked ogre himself.

Episode 1

"Aha!" says the great, wicked ogre, "it is a nice plump little pig that I have been wanting for my supper this many a day past. So you may just come along with me now."

"Oh, Master Ogre," squeaked the smallest of the little pigs in the smallest of voices—"oh, Master Ogre, don't eat me! There's a bigger pig back of me, and he will be along presently."

So the ogre let the smallest of the little pigs go, for he would rather have a larger pig if he could get it.

Episode 2

By and by came the second little pig. "Aha!" says the great, wicked ogre, "I have been wanting just such a little pig as you for my supper for this many a day past. So you may just come along with me now."

Oh, Master Ogre," says the middle-sized pig, in his middle-sized voice, "don't take me for your supper; there's a bigger pig than I am coming along presently. Just wait for him."

Well, the ogre was satisfied to do that; so he waited, and

Episode 3

by and by, sure enough, came the largest of the little pigs.

"And now," says the great, wicked ogre, "I will wait no longer, for you are just the pig I want for my supper."

But the largest of the little pigs had his wits about him, I can tell you. "Oh, very well," says he; "if I am the shoe that fits, there is no use in hunting for another; only, have you a roasted apple to put in my mouth when I am cooked? For no one ever heard of a little pig brought on the table without a roast apple in its mouth."

No; the ogre had no roasted apple.

Dear, dear! that was a great pity. If he would wait for a little while, the largest of the little pigs would run home and fetch one, and then things would be as they should.

Yes, the ogre was satisfied with that. So off ran the little pig, and the ogre sat down on a stone and waited for him.

Well, he waited and he waited and he waited and he waited, but not a tip of a hair of the little pig did he see that day, as you can guess without my telling you.

"And now," says the cock and the speckled hen and the black drake and the old gray goose who laid her eggs under the barn and had never been out into the world beyond the garden gate—"and now perhaps you will run out into the world and among ogres no more."

But no; that was not what the smallest of the three little pigs thought.

So out into the woods he went, and there he found all of the acorns that he wanted. But, on his way home, whom should he meet but the great, wicked ogre.

Episode 4

"Aha!" says the ogre, "and is that you?"

Oh, yes, it was nobody else; but had the ogre come across three fellows tramping about in the woods down yonder?

No, the ogre had met nobody in the woods that day.

"Dear, dear," says the smallest little pig, "but that is a pity, for those three fellows were three wicked robbers, and they have just hidden a mealbag full of money in that hole up in the tree yonder."

You can guess how the ogre pricked up his ears at this.

"Just wait," said he to the smallest little pig, "and I will be down again in a minute." So he laid his jacket to one side and up the tree he climbed to find that bag of money.

"Do you find the hole?" says the smallest of the little pigs.

Yes; the ogre had found the hole.

"And do you find the money?" says the smallest of the little pigs.

No; the ogre could find no money.

"Then good-by," says the smallest of the little pigs, and off he trotted home, leaving the ogre to climb down the tree again as he chose.

"And now, at least, you will go out into the woods no more," says the cock, the speckled hen, the black drake, and the gray goose.

Oh, well, there was no telling what the middle-sized little pig would do, for he also had a taste for acorns.

So out into the woods the middle-sized little pig went, and there he had all the acorns that he wanted.

But by and by the ogre came along. "Aha!" says he. "Now I have you for sure and certain." Episode 5

But the middle-sized little pig just stood and looked at a great rock just in front of him, with all of his might and main. "Sh-h-h-h-h-h!" says he, "I am not to be talked to or bothered now!"

Hoity-toity! And why was the middle-sized pig not to be talked to? That was what the ogre should like to know.

Oh, the middle-sized little pig was looking at what was going on under the great rock yonder, for he could see the little folk brewing more beer than thirty-seven men could drink.

So! Why, the ogre would like to see that for himself.

"Very well," says the middle-sized little pig, "there is nothing easier than to learn that trick! Just take a handful of leaves from yonder bush and rub them over your eyes, and then shut them tight and count fifty."

Well, the ogre would have a try at that. So he gathered a handful of the leaves and rubbed them over his eyes, just as the middle-sized pig had said.

"And now are you ready?" said the middle-sized little pig. Yes; the ogre was ready.

"Then shut your eyes and count," said the middle-sized little pig.

So the ogre shut them as tightly as he could and began to count, "One, two, three, four, five," and so on; and while he was counting, why, the little pig was running away home again.

By and by the ogre bawled out "*Fifty!!!*" and opened his eyes, for he was done. Then he saw not more, but less, than he had seen before, for the little pig was not there.

And now it was the largest of the three little pigs who began to talk about going out into the woods to look for acorns.

"You had better stay at home and take things as they come. The crock that goes often to the well gets broken at last"; that was what the cock, the speckled hen, the black drake, and the gray goose said.

But no; the little pig wanted to go out into the woods, and into the woods the little pig would go, ogre or no ogre.

After he had eaten all of the acorns that he wanted, he began to think of going home again, but just then the ogre came stumping along. "Aha!" says he, "we have met again, have we?"

Episode 6

"Yes," said the largest of the three little pigs, "we have. And I want to say that I could find no roast apple at home, and so I did not come back again."

Yes, yes, that was all very fine; but they should have a settling of old scores now. The largest of the three little pigs might just come along and be made into sausages.

Come, come! the ogre must not be too testy. If it were sausages that the ogre was after, maybe the pig could help him. Over home at the farm yonder was a storehouse filled with more sausages and good things than two men could count.

Well, the ogre and the largest of the three little pigs went off together. By and by they came to the storehouse. There was a window *just* large enough for the ogre to squeeze through without a button to spare in the size.

Then, dear, dear! how the ogre did stuff himself with the sausages and puddings and other good things.

By and by the little pig bawled out as loud as he could, *"Have you had enough yet?"*

"Hush-sh-sh-sh-sh-sh-sh!" says the ogre, "don't talk so loud, or you'll be rousing the folks and having them about our ears like a hive of bees."

"No," bawled the little pig, louder than before, "but tell me, *have* you had enough yet?"

"Yes, yes," says the ogre, "I have had almost enough, only be still about it!"

"Very well!" bawled the little pig, as loud as he could, "if you have had enough, and if you have eaten all of the sausages and all of the puddings you can stuff, it is about time that you were going, for here comes the farmer and two of his men."

When the ogre heard them coming, he felt sure that it was time that he was getting away home again, and so he tried to get out of the same window that he had gotten in a little while before. But he had stuffed himself with so much of the good

things that he had swelled like everything, and there he stuck in the storehouse window like a cork in a bottle and could budge neither one way nor the other; and that was a pretty pickle to be in.

"Oho!" says the farmer, "you were after my sausages and my puddings, were you? Then you will come no more."

And that was so; for when the farmer and his men were done with the ogre he never went into the woods again, for he could not.

The problem is solved. The story is over.

As for the three little pigs, they trotted away into the woods every day of their lives, for there was nobody nowadays to stop them from gathering all the acorns that they wanted.

PUSSY-WILLOWS

Spring, Spring,
everything
you do is new and shiny.
Who, who
teaches you
to think of things as tiny
as all those velvet
willow cats
in furry coats
and furry hats
astride a twig
like acrobats,
soft, and sleek, and shiny?

by Aileen Fisher

AFTERNOON ON A HILL

I will be the gladdest thing
   Under the sun!
I will touch a hundred flowers
   And not pick one.

I will look at cliffs and clouds
   With quiet eyes,
Watch the wind bow down the grass,
   And the grass rise.

And when lights begin to show
   Up from the town,
I will mark which must be mine,
   And then start down.

by Edna St. Vincent Millay

THE LAST WORD OF A BLUEBIRD

As I went out a Crow
In a low voice said 'Oh,
I was looking for you.
How do you do?
I just came to tell you
To tell Lesley (will you?)
That her little Bluebird
Wanted me to bring word
That the north wind last night
That made the stars bright
And made ice on the trough
Almost made him cough
His tail feathers off.
He just had to fly!
But he sent her Good-by,
And said to be good,
And wear her red hood,
And look for skunk tracks
In the snow with an ax—
And do everything!
And perhaps in the spring
He would come back and sing.'

by Robert Frost

Autumn

The morns are meeker than they were,
 The nuts are getting brown;
The berry's cheek is plumper,
 The rose is out of town.

The maple wears a gayer scarf,
 The field a scarlet gown.
Lest I should be old-fashioned,
 I'll put a trinket on.

by Emily Dickinson

Picture by Betty Fraser

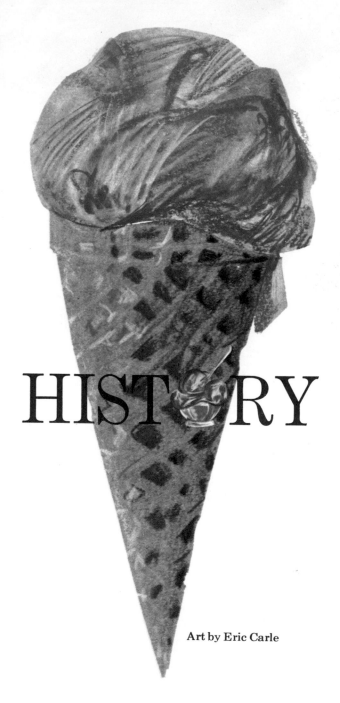

HIST RY

Art by Eric Carle

Bite by bite,
lick by lick,
Americans consume more
than four billion ice cream cones
each year.
The ice cream cone has become
a taken-for-granted part
of everyday life in America.
But it wasn't always so.
Until the turn of this century,
ice cream sold by street vendors
was served in glass dishes,
which required a great deal
of washing and care.
And customers were always
breaking the glasses
or walking away with them.
This unsatisfactory and expensive
means of serving ice cream
was changed in 1896
when the first
ice cream cone was invented.
The inventor
was an Italian immigrant,
named Italo Marchiony,
who sold ice cream
from a pushcart
in the streets of New York City.

Mr. Marchiony got tired
of washing his serving dishes
and buying new ones
to replace those
that had been broken,
so he decided to make
a new kind of container
for ice cream.
He baked a thin cooky
and rolled it up
into the shape of a cone.
Then he scooped ice cream
into the cone.

of the
ICE CREAM
CONE

His customers were delighted
with his new way
of serving ice cream,
and Mr. Marchiony was glad
to be free of dishes
and dishwashing.
These edible ice cream containers
became popular in New York.

They were called "toot" cones,
probably because
they resembled little horns.
Mr. Marchiony made a fortune
in New York
with his toot cones,
but somehow
the idea of the toot cone
never "caught on"
in the rest of the country.
It wasn't until
the St. Louis World's Fair in 1904
that the ice cream cone
was introduced to the world.
It so happened
that an ice cream vendor
at the Fair
was enjoying a brisk business
selling dishes of ice cream
for 5 cents and 10 cents.
One day he ran out of dishes
for ice cream
and didn't know what to do.
A Syrian waffle-maker
named Ernest Hamwi
had a waffle stand nearby.
When Mr. Hamwi
saw the problem
facing the ice cream vendor,
he suggested a simple solution.

He took one of his waffles,
which was very thin,
and rolled it up into a cone.
It cooled quickly
and became hard and dry.

Then the ice cream vendor
filled the cone with ice cream,
and his customers
"ate it up" so to speak.
The ice cream cone
was on its way to becoming
an all-American treat.

The ice cream cone customers
at the St. Louis World's Fair
loved the cone so much
that they took the idea
back to their home towns
all across the country,
and before long
ice cream vendors
were selling the waffle-cones
at fair grounds,
carnivals, beaches,
amusement parks,
and, of course,
in all the neighborhood
ice cream parlors.

Soon the national demand
for the cones
became so great
that the old method
of rolling cones by hand
proved too slow.
In order to supply
the growing demand,
machines were built in 1905
that could make
1,500 cones a day.
Cone-making machines
have been greatly improved
since then.
Now there are machines that,
with the press of a button,
automatically produce in a day
150,000 cones by themselves.

There are two kinds
of cone-making machines.
One is called
a baking-and-rolling machine,
which first bakes the waffles
and then automatically
rolls them into cones.
The other is called
a split-mold machine.
It pours waffle batter
into a cone-shaped mold
and then bakes the batter.
After the cone cools and hardens,
the mold automatically
comes apart,
and the cone is removed.

Strawberry?
Vanilla?
Double-decker?
Triple-decker?
What's your favorite kind
of ice cream cone?
Make mine a triple-decker —
a scoop of chocolate,
then a scoop of pineapple sherbet,
and crown that with
a scoop of peppermint stick.
Wow!

We're right behind you, Charlie Brown

An editorial feature,
with cartoons by Charles Schulz

Americans love popcorn,
hot dogs, ice cream cones—
and Charlie Brown.
He and his friends
are more popular today
than they have ever been
in seventeen years
of their lives.
Isn't it interesting

that these comic-strip characters
never grow older
and never really change.
Charlie is still
losing ball games,
one after another.
At last count
he had just lost
999 ball games in a row

Lucy is just as grumpy
as she ever was.
She "hollers" so loud
that she can be heard
for blocks around,
but this is no louder
than she "hollered" yesterday
or ten years ago.
Her little brother, Linus,
still carries his baby blanket
around and sucks his thumb.
He probably will never
outgrow those habits.

Snoopy, the dog,
never does anything right,
but nobody wants
to change Snoopy.
They like him just as he is.
Actually, there's much good
that can be said about the way
a comic is put together.
For one thing,
you don't have any trouble
knowing what's happening.
The pictures tell the story.

When words are spoken,
a "balloon" shows
who is doing the talking.

When a person shouts,
the words get larger
and blacker,
helping the reader know
how they sound.

Moreover, a comic story
is short.
In five minutes, or less,
you've been in and out
of the story
unless you are reading
one of your favorite comic books.

And finally,
the comic characters never change.
They become old friends
whom we love,
even though we know their faults
and what they will be doing
tomorrow.

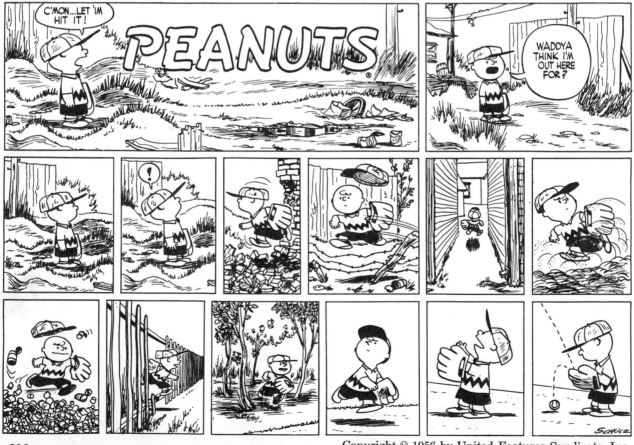

plugging into meanings

Sometimes when you are reading,
do you feel like a wired-up lion,
who has been trained to read every page
just so he can "come up" with the author's ideas?
Well, don't.
Reading is like a telephone conversation.
Your ideas are equally as important as the author's.
There has to be a party at each end of the "line"
to make the conversation come alive.

An essay by Bill Martin, Jr.,
sculpture by Ralph Moxcey,
photo by Bob O'Shaugnessy

The author is talking to you through the printed page.
You talk with him by thinking about what he is saying
and deciding whether or not you agree with him.
Every good reader I know talks his way through books.
He and the author become quite chummy agreeing and disagreeing,
and in other ways "brushing off" on each other.
He never counts a book as being a good book
unless it helped him know more about himself
as well as about the author and their separate ways of thinking.

Think back on the story, "Billy Had a System," page 52.
Your experience with boys who sometimes are forced
to go to parties when they would rather be playing ball
may have put you in perfect agreement with the author
who wrote this as an amusing story.
On the other hand, if you are a person
whose party has been wrecked by boys like Billy and Fats,
you may have found nothing funny in the story at all.
In fact, it may have been distasteful to you to read the story
because it brought up memories of a washed-out party.
Then, if your teacher happens to ask you
what kind of story this was and expected you to say *humorous*,
you would have appeared to be wrong
if you said it was an *unpleasant* story.
The trick is to learn enough about yourself
and about the author to be able to say,

Well, the author thinks this is a funny story, but I don't.

An answer of this kind shows that you have "plugged in"
both to the author's meanings and to your own meanings.

Some readers plug into their own meanings and feelings
so rapidly and so heatedly
that they are not in a mood to give the author a chance to talk.
If you want to be a reader who can "take in" new meanings
even when they are distasteful or uncomfortable to you,
the best advice I can give is, first of all,
to know what the book really means to you.
Once you know where you stand in relation to the ideas
and feelings expressed in the book,
you won't find it uncomfortable to "listen"
to the author's point of view.
In fact, you may even find it exciting.
The wonderful thing about reading
is that no two of us think and feel exactly alike.
It would be a pretty dull world if every book echoed
only your way of thinking and feeling.
This would never give you a chance to learn anything new.
The next time you find yourself reading a book you don't like
or getting into a serious discussion with a person
whose ideas you don't like
or watching a TV show with characters you don't like,
remember, it's a two-way telephone conversation.
You can "plug in" to their meanings and still like your own.
Your point of view counts just as much
as that of the person on the other end of the line—
but no more than that.
He, too, has a point of view.
The better you understand what that point of view is,
the better prepared you are to decide
whether or not you agree with it.

operation moonbean!

a picture for storytelling

by Earl Thollander

Language
works in chunks
of meaning. The first
chunk interlocks with the
second, with the third, and so on,
to the end of the sentence.

Little Thomas was glad when he and his family moved

The memory of the first chunk
of meaning is stored in
your mind as you move
from it to the
second and
third.

Each chunk has its own meaning,
but it also becomes part of
a larger meaning that is
developing as you
read farther
into the
sentence.

into a neighborhood where there were lots of kids,

Little Thomas Punch-the-Pig

By Bill Martin, Jr.,
with drawings by Leo and Diane Dillon

It
now has
been several
seconds since you
started reading this
sentence. So the sentence
is actually moving through time.

even though   *it meant that he always had to be "it"*

The sentence began on the last
page. It will continue
onto the next page.
So the sentence
is moving
through
space.

when they met in the orchard after school

As
you read
to the end of the
sentence, you, too, have
moved through time and space.
Reading is like riding in a car.
You move from one chunk of meaning to
another to arrive at a new destination.

═══ *to play a game of Punch-the-Pig and Kick-the-Can.* ═══

With this last chunk of meaning, the
sentence itself becomes complete.
All of the chunks now form
into a larger and some-
what new meaning.
And you're ready
to move into
the next
sentence.

213

The Web of Winter

A story by Esther MacBain Meeks,
water color illustration by Willi Baum

Bill stood by the marsh
watching small flocks
of birds
looking for food.
The birds darted
among the dry reeds
and barren branches,
pecking at shriveled berries
and pods
to get at their hidden seeds.
Bill wondered
how the birds kept warm
in the stinging cold.
At last he ran out
on the ice and slid,
making great long tracks.
He alternately ran and slid
across the marsh
until he came
to the *turn-around*—
an empty barrel
frozen into the ice.
He sat down on the barrel
to fasten his boot.
His breath came out
on the cold air
in thin white puffs.

*This quietly moving story has
all the tenderness of a boy's love
for a wild creature. It is told
against a background of a family's love for one another and
for life itself. The story is so
simple that you may not at first
sense its impact, but we're guessing that after you have read it,
you'll never forget "The Web of
Winter."*

The wind
grew suddenly quiet.
That's when Bill
first heard the sound.
It was so faint
that he was not sure
he had heard it.
The sound came again,
high and thin.
"Quick..."
Bill listened.
It came again.
"Quick...quick."
Could it be the ice
breaking under his weight?
He looked carefully.
No, the ice was hard
and firm.
"Quick...quick."
What could the sound be?
Bill knew the call
of the winter birds—
the whistle of a cardinal,
the chatter of a blue jay,
the *cheep* of a sparrow.
It wasn't a bird he knew,
and it didn't sound
like the cry of an animal.
"Quick...quick."
The sound floated again
over the marsh.
Bill rose to follow it.

Picking his way
among the weeds
and tall grasses,
he came to the edge
of the marsh.
He pushed the reeds aside
and listened.
All was silent.
He bent his head,
waiting for the sound
to come again.
"Quick...quick."

"I'm coming," he answered,
making his way
through the brush.
Every few steps he stopped,
waiting for the voice
to guide him.
But the voice
did not come again.
The sun set behind the willows.
It grew late and dark.
Bill waited
as long as he could.

Finally he had to leave.
It was suppertime
and his mother
expected him home.

The next day, after school,
Bill returned to the marsh
for skating.
He carried
his skates and a broom
on his sled
and pulled them out

to the center of the marsh
where the ice
could be cleared
for skating.
He sat down
on the sled
to put on his skates.
Then he took the broom
and swept the snow
off the ice,
leaving the surface
smooth for skating.

He found an old tomato can and batted it before him
as he skated around, using the broom as a hockey stick.
Then he dropped the broom and raced around and around
the turn-around barrel. His quick turns on the ice
made a deep grating sound and threw up a cloud
of white dust behind him. He practiced
all sorts of turns and skated with abandon—
forward, backward, stopping, starting,
turning, gliding, fast, slow.
He was skating near the turn-around barrel
when he heard the sound again.

"Quick . . . quick."
It came the same as yesterday. Bill cocked
his head and listened.

"Quick . . ."
The sound wasn't far away. Bill skated quietly
toward it.

"Quick . . . quick."
Now he heard quite clearly. The snow
was thicker at the edge of the marsh
and was too rough for skating. He had to walk
on his skates, leaving short thin tracks behind him.
Then suddenly, the same as the day before,
the sound stopped.

Bill stood still. He listened and watched.
After a bit, he kneeled down and called softly,
"Quick . . . quick . . ."

He waited for an answer. None came.

He called again, "Quick."

There was no reply. He listened a long time
and stood up to go. That is when he found it.
In a tangle of dry weeds, he saw a duck
huddled in the snow. It was sitting so still
it looked like a decoy.

"Hello," Bill said, bending down.

The bird trembled and fluttered its wings.
It was a young duck.

"It's too cold here for you, Quick-quick.
Why haven't you flown away?"

The duck beat its wings frantically.
The snow flew, but the bird could not. It was
caught in the ice. Bill knew that birds often rested
in icy water, but he had never heard
of anything like this. The water had frozen firmly
around the duck's feet.

Bill gently took the bird in his hands.
He tried to lift, but the ice held the duck
as tightly as it held the turn-around barrel.

"Don't worry," Bill said. "I'll get you out."

It was easier said than done. The duck
was not only trapped, it was cold and hungry.
Bill broke off some grasses and piled them
in front of the bird where it could get
at the seeds. But Quick-quick
refused the food.

"Maybe he's too weak to eat," Bill thought.

The duck cried a low pitiful sound.
Bill feared the duck was nearly dead.
There was no time to run two miles home for help.
He himself must act—and quickly.

"Here," he said, loosening his scarf
and wrapping it around the duck. "This will warm
you a little."

The wind whipped the scarf out of his hands,
but he grabbed it and wrapped it around
the captive bird.

Now what to do?

Bill ran for his sled. He had seen men
make wind shelters when they were ice-fishing,
so he propped the sled up to shelter the duck
while he tried to free it.

Bill took off his skates
and quickly put on his boots,
He used the blade
of one skate as a knife,
trying to cut through
the thick layer of ice.
He cut a circle
around the bird.
Now, the real work began.
He retraced the marks
again and again,
each time cutting
a little deeper in the ice.
This was the way
Bill and his dad
made fishing holes
in the ice,
only they used a hatchet
and an ice pick.
Bill chopped at the ice.
He grew warmer and warmer.
He also grew
more and more tired.
Frequently he had to stop
to rest his aching arms.
He worked so hard
that he didn't think
about the time.
The sun was low
behind the willow trees
at the edge of the marsh
before he noticed
the darkness.

Someone called. "Bill! Hey, Bill!
Are you down there?" It was his sister.

"Here I am, Thelma! Over here!"

Thelma came toward him through the
tall weeds.

"A duck's caught here in the ice,"
Bill shouted. "I'm cutting him free."

"Where have you been? Mom's worried silly,"
Thelma said.

"I've been here," Bill said. "I can't leave
or this duck will die."

Thelma saw the bird now and how Bill was trying
to free it. "It's dangerous to cut holes in the ice,"
she said. "You should *never never* do it
when you're alone."

"I know," Bill answered. "But it's shallow here
and near the shore. Besides, there wasn't time
to get help."

223

"Where's the other skate?"
Thelma asked.
Without waiting
for an answer,
she found it
and started to work,
using the tip of the blade
like an ice pick.
She chopped at the ice
with the skate
and gouged out
good-sized chunks.
"Good work, Thelma,"
Bill said.
"We'll have this duck
free in no time."
They chopped and chopped,
but it was hard going,
and very slow.
Soon another voice
came out of the dusk.
"Thelma! Bill!"
Mother had come
to look for them.
"We can't come,"
Thelma called back.
"Bill found a duck
frozen onto the ice.
We are trying
to rescue it."
"Found what?"
Mother called.

Mother scolded as she came across the ice. Then she saw the bird huddled under the scarf, and her attitude changed. "It's dangerous to cut holes in the ice, and you should *never never* do it without a grownup along."

"Yeah, Mom," Bill said. "You sound just like Thelma. She said the same thing. But there wasn't time."

"Well, I can help, too. Hand me the broom." Mother said. She began sweeping the ice chips away from the crack where Bill and Thelma were chopping.

A truck came bumping along the shore road, its headlights shining through the weeds. It was Father. He pulled the truck to a stop.

His voice rang out in the dark. "Bill! . . . Thelma! . . . Mother!"

"Over here," Mother answered.

Father got out of the truck and came to see what was doing. When he saw them chopping, he scolded, "Why didn't you call me? It's dangerous to cut holes in the ice. You should *never* do it without a man around."

"Here we go again," Bill said without looking up.

Father looked at the duck,
then at the circle.
"I'll get my tools," he said.
Father went back
to the truck
and returned with a hammer
and a jack handle.
Soon the ice chips were flying.
The duck pulled
its head back in alarm.
Now it was very dark
and hard to see.
"That's enough," Bill said
as he tested the ice
and felt it give.
Father tapped along the circle
with the hammer.
The tapping opened the crack.
The ice cake,
still holding the bird,
broke loose.
Bill and Father
carefully lifted
the small island of ice
and carried it,
bird and all,
to the truck.
Bill laid his hand
on the bird's breast
and felt its heart fluttering.
"He's still alive," he said.

Quick-quick,
his feet still frozen
in the cake of ice,
was loaded into the truck.
Bill and Thelma sat beside him
on the trip home.
The duck was placed
in the bathtub,
and Bill drew warm water
to hurry the thawing of the ice.
"Quick . . . quick . . ."
Quick-quick seemed
to know that
he had been saved.
His voice was faint,
but, at least Bill knew
he was still alive.
Bill hung over the edge
of the bathtub,
encouraging the duck
with kind talk
and offers of food.
By morning
he was paddling around
in the bathtub
as if he enjoyed
his new home.
"Quick, quick, quack!
Quick, quick, quack!"
He fluttered his wings
and splashed water
over the floor.

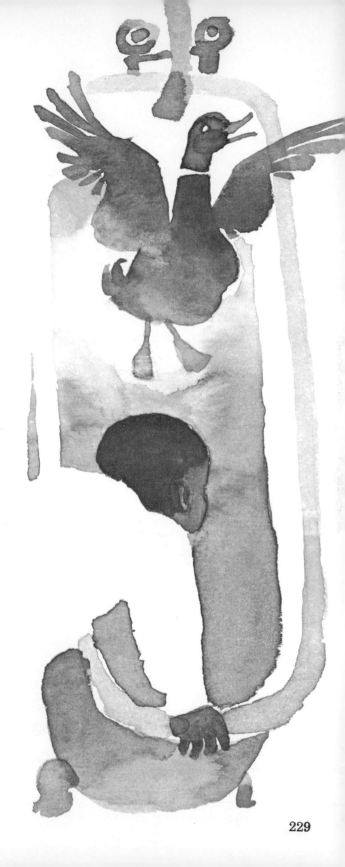

The next week, after he was strong enough to go on his way,
Bill and Thelma took him back to the marsh and set him free.
Out he flew over the ice and, without turning back,
disappeared over the woods and over the hill.
Now, in fall and spring when the birds fly overhead,
Bill still watches the ducks that come to the marsh.
He listens for Quick-quick, knowing that the bird
may never remember him, but he will never forget
the bird and his *quick...quick...*and *quick, quick, quack!*

Cardinal

Chickadee

How Birds Keep Warm in Winter

When you see a chickadee huddled on a snowy branch or a duck swimming in icy water, do you wonder how birds keep warm in winter?

A bird has several layers of winter feathers to keep him warm. Next to his skin is a blanket of filmy feathers called *down* and some fluffy body feathers. This blanket of feathers traps the bird's body heat in millions of tiny air pockets, keeping it warm. The bird's outer feathers are staggered like shingles on a roof to keep out the rain and snow. The strong outer feathers can withstand all kinds of wind and weather.

A bird regulates his body temperature by changing the position of his feathers. When he is perched or sleeping in the cold, he fluffs out the feathers to trap the warm air near his skin. When he is too warm and wants to cool off, he hugs his feathers close to his body to squeeze out the warm air.

An article
written and illustrated
by Bernard Martin

Pigeon

Crop

Stomach

Gizzard

Intestines

You may be surprised to discover that a bird has a "furnace" that makes heat to keep him warm.

The bird's stomach is his furnace. When a pigeon eats a seed, a wonderful process begins within its body. The seed is stored in the bird's crop until it is needed for heat and energy. Then the seed goes into the stomach where it is softened by gastric juices. Later the seed moves into the gizzard where it is ground by strong, gritty muscles into fine particles that can be digested easily. These fine particles, like fiercely burning wood or coal, flow through the small intestines. They are absorbed by the intestinal walls and released into the blood stream, to be used by the body as heat and power. Your body digests food for heat and energy in much the same way.

A bird that lives in the snow and cold must eat from dawn until dusk to "keep his furnace roaring." The fuel burns quickly, and if the "fire" goes out, the bird will freeze to death.

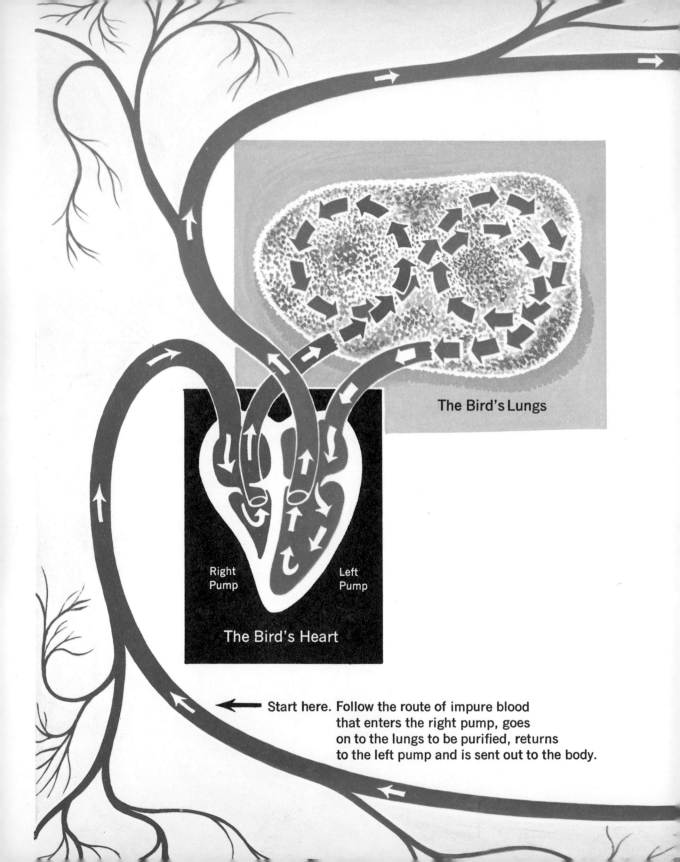

The Bird's Lungs

Right Pump

Left Pump

The Bird's Heart

Start here. Follow the route of impure blood
that enters the right pump, goes
on to the lungs to be purified, returns
to the left pump and is sent out to the body.

Have you ever held a bird in your hands?
Did you wonder why its body felt so warm
and why its heart was beating so rapidly?
Did you think it was frightened?
Perhaps it was a little frightened,
but a bird's heart always beats at a rapid rate.
The fast-beating heart keeps the bird's body temperature high
and helps to keep the bird snug and warm
during cold weather. When a pigeon is resting,
his heart races along at 192 beats a minute,
pumping warm blood through every part of his body
and keeping his body temperature at 110 degrees.
A canary's heart beats 1000 times a minute!
An endless river of energy flows from a bird's heart
through his body. The bird's heart has
two strong pumps. The right pump of the heart
sends blood to the lungs where it is purified
with oxygen. The purified blood is then returned
to the left pump of the heart
and forced on through other parts of the bird's body.

A bird also has another way to help keep himself warm in winter.

He oils his feathers, squeezing oil from a gland on his back. This waterproofs his feathers, providing him with a raincoat for protection from cold and rainy weather.

There is a way that you can help keep birds warm in winter. By seeing to it that the birds near your home have plenty to eat, you can help "keep their furnaces roaring" and their bodies warm in winter.

Titmouse

Part II
responding to reading

Just reading
is not enough
If reading is . . . .
of any importance, it must
cause you to stir, . .
to feel, ...
to think, ...
to respond, . .
to get a larger . . . .
view of the world . . . .
This half of *Sounds of Mystery* suggests   . . . .
some ways that you can respond to reading: . . . .
. . . . by reading aloud . . . . storytelling . . . .
choral reading . . . . creative dramatics . . . .
wondering about words . . . . pondering ideas . . .
and . . . . thinking of possibilities . . . .
making judgments about the things you have read. . .
You may have wondered why your teachers . . . .
sometimes suggest that you make . . . .
a play of a story . . . .
that you have read . . . .
or that you ar- . . . .
range a choral . . .
reading of a . . .
favorite poem.
It is their way of
helping you find new
meanings in
what
you have
read.

An announcement by Bill Martin, Jr.

239

An essay by Bill Martin, Jr.

Once upon a time...
Is there a more beautiful phrase in our language?
The very sound of it makes us forget our cares
and sit back, pleasantly expecting to hear something worthwhile.
The storyteller, for as long as man can remember,
has always been a welcomed guest at the fireside
and at the crossroads. The sound of his voice
and the spell of his stories bring new hope
and new dreams to those who listen.

Lucky are the people who have had a storyteller in their lives.
Perhaps it was a grandmother or a teacher or a friend.
The storyteller helped them experience new joys and wonderings
as his tales unfolded. There are two ways of telling a story.

One is to read the story aloud from the printed page.
The storyteller knows the story well and enjoys reading it
to others. He is sure of the words,
the way the sentences string together,
and the places in the story where the suspense is the greatest.

On the other hand, stories are sometimes told by heart.
The storyteller may be making up the story as he goes along,
and he may be telling in his own way a story that he has read
or heard. If you are interested in telling stories by heart,
you can help yourself by jotting down the sequence of events
in the story and practice telling it often enough
so that you find the best ways to say it.

Don't have the idea that once a story is told,
it is over and done with. You can tell the same story
many, many times, to different audiences on different occasions.
People also enjoy hearing certain stories over and over again.
This makes the time spent in preparing to tell a story
well worthwhile.

In this section and elsewhere in *Sounds of Mystery*
are many stories and poems and songs
that you will find worthy of storytelling.
You also will find pictures that invite you
to weave a written story. You may be especially interested
to know that "Rikki-tikki-tavi" (page 258)
is one storyteller's way of retelling a classic story.
You may enjoy comparing the telling of "Rikki-tikki-tavi"
in this book, with the original story
found in *The Jungle Book* by Rudyard Kipling.

The Conjure Wives

Once on a time,
when a Halloween night came
on the dark o' the moon,
a lot o' old conjure wives
was a-sittin' by the fire
an' a-cookin' a big supper
for theirselves.
The wind was a-howlin' 'round
like it does on Halloween nights,
an' the old conjure wives
they hitched theirselves
up to the fire
an' talked about the spells
they was a-goin' to weave
long come midnight.

a folktale for reading aloud, with pictures by Albert Pucci

By an' by
there come a-knockin' at the door.
   "Who's there?"
called an old conjure wife.

   "Who-o? Who-o?
     One who is hungry
     and cold,"
said a voice.

Then the old conjure wives
they all burst out laughin'
an' they called out:
   "We's a-cookin' for ourselves.
   Who'll cook for you?
   Who? Who?"

The voice didn't say nothin',
but the knockin' just kept on.

   "Who's that a-knockin'?"
called out another conjure wife.
   "Who? Who?"

Then there come a whistlin',
wailin' sound:
   "Let me in, do-o-o-o!
     I'se cold thro-o-o-o
     an' thro-o-o-o,
     an' I'se hungry too-o-o!"

Then the old conjure wives
they all burst out laughin',
an' they commenced
to sing out:

"Git along, do!
We's a-cookin' for ourselves.
Who'll cook for you?
Who? Who?"

An' the voice didn't say nothin',
but the knockin' just kept on.

Then the old conjure wives
began to get scared-like,
an' one of 'em says,
"Let's give it somethin'
an' get it away
before it spoils our spells."

An' the voice didn't say nothin',
but the knockin' just kept on.
Then the conjure wives
they took the littlest piece of dough,

as big as a pea,
an' they put it in the fry pan.
An' the voice didn't say nothin',
but the knockin' just kept on.
An' when they put the dough
in the fry pan,
it begun to swell an' swell,
an' it swelled over the fry pan
an' it swelled over the top
o' the stove
an' it swelled out on the floor.
An' the voice didn't say nothin',
but the knockin' just kept on.
Then the old conjure wives
got scared
an' they ran for the door,
an' the door was *shut tight.*
An' the voice didn't say nothin',
but the knockin' just kept on.
An' then the dough
it swelled an' it swelled
all over the floor
an' it swelled up into the chairs.

An' the old conjure wives
they climbed up
on the backs of the chairs
an' they were scareder
and scareder.
An' they called out,
  "Who's that a-knockin'
   at the door? Who? Who?"

an' they kept a-callin',
  "Who's that a-knockin'?
   Who? Who?"

An' the voice didn't say nothin',
but the knockin' just kept on.
An' the dough kept a-swellin'
an' a-swellin',
an' the old conjure wives
begun to scrooge up
smaller an' smaller,
an' their eyes
got bigger an' bigger
with scaredness,

An' then the knockin' stopped,
and the voice called out,
*"Fly out the window, do!
  There's no more house for you!"*

An' the old conjure wives
they spread their wings
an' they flew out the windows
an' off into the woods,
all a-callin',

Only on a Halloween night
you don't want to go
'round the old owls,
because *then*
they turns to old conjure wives
a-weavin' their spells.

"Who'll cook for you?
Who? Who?"

An' now if you go into the woods
in the dark o' the moon,
you'll see
the old conjure wife owls
an' hear 'em callin',
  "Who'll cook for you?
  Who-o! Who-o!"

J.KUNZ

Trees Alone Do Not Make a Forest

A forest is more than a spread of trees. It is a "town," a community with a vast population of animal and plant life.

The members of the forest community could not survive without each other. They depend on each other for food. The plants wage a constant battle among themselves for the sunlight, soil, water and minerals necessary for life and growth. The animals, too, try to eat without being eaten.

The death of every plant and every animal feeds new forest life. Everything in the forest is part of the endless pattern of *growth and decay*, of *life and death* in the forest.

Forest Life in the Treetops

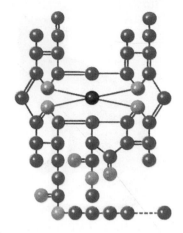

Leaves give life to the forest. Green leaves on trees, vines, shrubs and bushes make plant food. And in doing so, they provide food for all animals in the world.

This represents part of the atoms in a chlorophyll molecule. Chlorophyll is the green substance in leaves that enables them to combine water from the soil with carbon and oxygen from the air to produce the plant food called glucose.

Birds, too, live in the branches of trees. They feed on insects and prevent great armies of insects from destroying the trees. However, not all birds live on insects. Owls, hawks and eagles feed upon toads and squirrels and other small animals of the forest.

Squirrels not only live in trees but also feed upon their seeds. This is small loss to the trees, and being carried away by squirrels and other animals is an important way for seeds to get scattered throughout the forest.

The forest food cycle begins with leaves and ends with such animals as foxes, bears and wolves. These animals eat other animals of the forest. Their only enemies are dogs and man, disease and starvation.

Some insects help the life of the forest by carrying pollen from flower to flower. However, many insects are harmful, feeding upon the leaves of forest plants. If it were not for birds and toads, insects would soon destroy the forest.

Toads and frogs feed upon the millions of insects that live on the forest floor. But, in turn, toads and frogs often become food for other animals. The backs of many toads are covered with poison glands that cause pain or death to animals that try to eat them.

Plants such as mushrooms and toadstools do not produce their own food because they do not have leaves. These scavenger plants, known as fungi, feed on dead plants and thereby help rid the forest of rubbish.

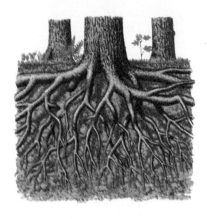

Forest Life Underground

The food cycle of the forest begins and ends in the soil of the forest floor. The roots of plants take water from the soil to be used in making plant food. The roots also anchor the trees and help keep soil from being washed away.

Earthworms help the forest by plowing the soil in search for food. They dig passages that allow air and water to pass freely through the earth. Earthworms are just one of hundreds of kinds of animals that live on the forest floor.

Forest Life Inside Things

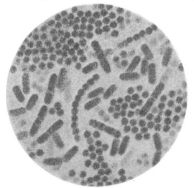

Many insects in their larval (worm) stage feed upon the wood of living trees, often destroying them. Other insects eat dead wood, thereby causing the wood to crumble and decay. This enriches the soil and helps clear away the rubbish in the forest.

Bacteria live in dead things like trees and leaves and animals and cause the dead matter to decay. The decay enriches the soil which helps things grow. And so, life in the forest is renewed by decay, year after year after year.

Come Dance with Me

Here is a story that may explain how a dance called the merengue
originated. It also is a story that lends itself to acting out.

Once upon a time in a country
where the people were fond
of music and dancing,
there lived a prince
who was the best dancer of all.
He moved to the music
like a soaring bird
and, seemingly, never tired.
Then one day the Prince was injured
in the jungle
and, thereafter,
walked with a stiffness
in his right knee.
The Prince grieved
that this should happen to him,
for his dancing days were over.
His father, the King,
shared his son's grief
and sent to every corner
of the land,
seeking someone to help.
Many came but none succeeded,
and, at last, the Prince lost hope
that he would ever dance again.
Then, one day, a young girl
came from the far mountains
to give her help to the Prince.

"Are you a physician?"
   he asked gloomily,
   knowing that she was not.
"How can you help me."

"I am not a physician," she said,
"but I, too, like to dance.
   Come, dance with me?"

"But my knee is stiff," he said.
"My dancing days are over."

"Have you not noticed?"
   replied the girl.
"I, too, have a stiff knee."
   The Prince, at first,
   was taken back.
Then he rose stiffly
   and led her to the village square
   to join in the dancing.
The townspeople stopped short
   to see their prince dancing again.
They were so proud of him
   that they wanted to cheer.
Instead, so that the Prince
   and his partner
   would not feel shy,
   they, too, joined in the dance,
   all dancing with stiff right knees.

A story by Bill Martin, Jr.

A
TRUE
FRIEND
IS
LIKE
HAVING

AN
EXTRA
PAIR
OF
HANDS

A proverb, designed by Art Ritter

Three Pictures Tell a Prairie Story

Here are three paintings
by the well-known painter
Harvey Dunn,
who loved the prairies
and prairie people.
He was a prairie boy himself.
You can read his pictures
like you read a book,
for the pictures are alive
with prairie experiences.
In looking at these pictures,
it is useful to ask,

"How do the lines and colors
and shapes tell me
what Harvey Dunn wanted me
to know about the prairie?"
How does the grass
in the first picture
tell you that the land
is rich for farming?
How does the girl's hair
in the last picture
tell that the wind is blowing?

Alligator on the Escalator

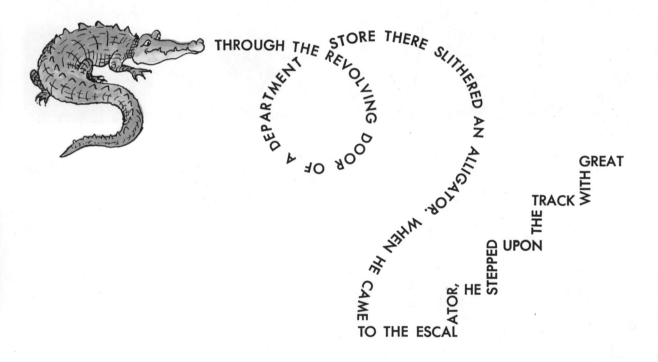

THROUGH THE STORE THERE SLITHERED AN ALLIGATOR, WHEN HE CAME TO THE ESCALATOR, HE STEPPED UPON THE TRACK WITH GREAT ATOR OF A DEPARTMENT REVOLVING DOOR OF A DEPARTMENT

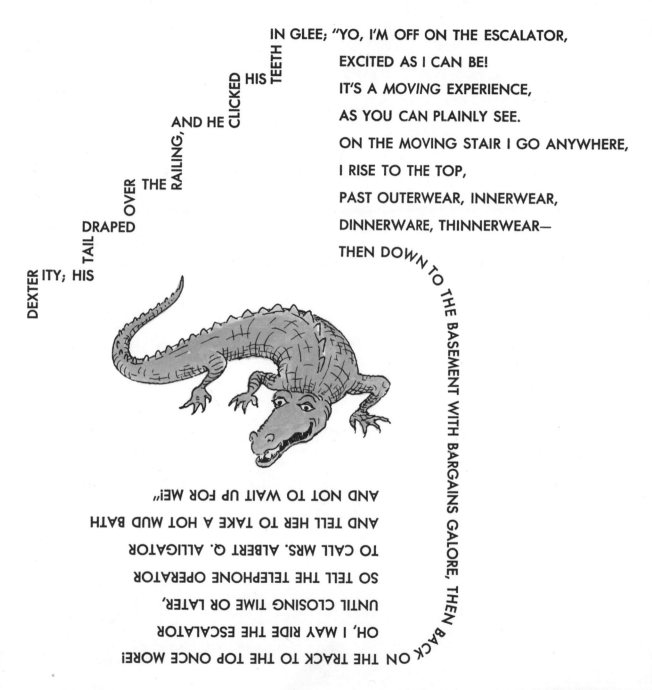

DEXTER ITY; HIS TAIL DRAPED OVER THE RAILING, AND HE CLICKED HIS TEETH IN GLEE; "YO, I'M OFF ON THE ESCALATOR,

EXCITED AS I CAN BE!

IT'S A MOVING EXPERIENCE,

AS YOU CAN PLAINLY SEE.

ON THE MOVING STAIR I GO ANYWHERE,

I RISE TO THE TOP,

PAST OUTERWEAR, INNERWEAR,

DINNERWARE, THINNERWEAR—

THEN DOWN TO THE BASEMENT WITH BARGAINS GALORE, THEN BACK ON THE TRACK TO THE TOP ONCE MORE!

OH, I MAY RIDE THE ESCALATOR

UNTIL CLOSING TIME OR LATER,

SO TELL THE TELEPHONE OPERATOR

TO CALL MRS. ALBERT Q. ALLIGATOR

AND TELL HER TO TAKE A HOT MUD BATH

AND NOT TO WAIT UP FOR ME!"

by Eve Merriam,
pictures by Kelly Oechsli

One of the great stories
of all time
by Rudyard Kipling,
adapted by Bill Martin, Jr.,
with drawings by Mel Hunter

RIKKI-
TIKKI-
TAVI

Teddy found Rikki-tikki-tavi

in a ditch one summer morning after a heavy rain.

Rikki-tikki-tavi's name is pronounced
to rhyme with Ricky and Davey.

The rising water had washed the little

mongoose from its burrow, and Teddy had carried

A mongoose, when fighting, stands
on his hind legs like a kangaroo.

it home inside his shirt. Teddy and

his father and his mother were English. They were

A mongoose has but one purpose
in life — to fight and kill snakes.

living in India where Teddy's father

was doing business for the King. Teddy begged

Rikki was a brave little animal, even when he met a black king cobra.

to keep the little mongoose for a pet,

but Teddy's mother was fearful about having a

The name of Nag, the king cobra, is pronounced with a broad *a* like in *father*.

mongoose in the house. When Teddy's

father came home that evening, he reassured his

Nagaina's name has 3 *a* sounds: first, a broad *a*; second, a long *a*; third, the schwa sound.

wife that a mon- goose would be good

protection against the danger of snakes in the

The name of Darzee, the tailor-bird, is pronounced to rhyme with Marcie.

garden, and so  Teddy was given

permission to keep the homeless little mongoose.

Rikki-tikki meets Nag.

Every morning
after his breakfast
of bits of banana and boiled egg,
Rikki-tikki-tavi
scuttled around the bushes
in the garden
just to see what was to be seen.
He was rather like a little cat
in his fur and tail,
but quite like a weasel
in his head and habits.
His eyes
and the end of his restless nose
were pink;
he could scratch himself
anywhere he pleased
with any leg, front or back;
he could fluff up his tail
till it looked like a bottle-brush;
and his war cry
as he scuttled
through the long grass
was:
Rikk-tikk-tikki-tikki-tchk!

One morning
when Rikki-tikki-tavi
was in the garden,
he heard Darzee, the tailor-bird,
sitting on her nest
in the pine tree, crying.
A tailor-bird looks and sounds
something like a catbird.

Rikki-tikki stood up
on his hind legs and asked:
"What's the matter with you?"

"Oh, Rikki,
a terrible thing has happened.
One of my babies
fell out of the nest yesterday
and Nag ate him."

"Hm-m!" said Rikki-tikki,
"That is very sad —
but I am a stranger here.
Who is Nag?"

Just then the little mongoose
heard a cold, horrid sound
behind him
that made him jump
two feet into the air
and whirl around.

Inch by inch
out of the grass
rose up the head
and spread hood
of Nag, the black king cobra,
who was five feet long
from tongue to tail.

When he had lifted
one third of himself
clear of the ground,
he stayed balancing to and fro
exactly as a dandelion tuft
balances in the wind,
and he looked at Rikki-tikki
with wicked eyes
that never changed expression,
whatever the snake
might have been thinking.

"Who is Nag?" he said.
"I am Nag.
Look, and be afraid!"

It is true
that Rikki-tikki was afraid
for a moment;
but it was impossible
for him to stay frightened
for any length of time.

Though Rikki-tikki had never met
a live cobra before,
his mother had fed him
on dead ones,
and he knew
that a grown mongoose's
business in life
was to fight and eat snakes.
Nag knew that, too, and
at the bottom of his cold heart,
he, too, was afraid.

Suddenly
Darzee, the tailor-bird,
who was sitting on her nest
in the pine tree
watching the two below,
cried out:
"Behind you, Rikki!
Look behind you!"

Fortunately
Rikki-tikki knew better
than to waste time in looking.
He jumped up into the air
as high as he could go,
and just under him
whizzed the black blur
of another snake.

It was another cobra,
Nagaina,
Nag's wicked mate.
She had crept up behind Rikki
as he was talking
to make an end of him;
and he heard her savage hiss
as the stroke missed.
Rikki-tikki came down
almost across her back.
If he had been
a wise, full-grown mongoose,
he would have known
that then was the time
to scramble up the snake's back
and to break her neck
by biting sharply
just above her spread hood.
He bit, indeed,
in the middle of her back
where it did little damage.
Then he jumped clear
of the snake to avoid
the terrible lashing return-stroke
of the cobra,
which sometimes can be
just as deadly to a mongoose
as the cobra's bite.
Nagaina was left torn and angry.

Now it is said that
when a cobra misses its stroke,
it never says anything
or gives any sign
of what it means to do next.
Without a word
Nagaina slithered off
through the tall grass
to reconnoiter,
and Nag followed her.

Nag and Nagaina plan their attack.

That night
Teddy carried Rikki-tikki
off to bed with him.
Rikki-tikki was too well bred
to bite or scratch,
but as soon as Teddy was asleep,
he went off for his night walk
around the house.

Instantly Rikki-tikki knew
that something was strange
about this night.
The house was as still as still,
but he thought he could hear
the faintest scratch-scratch
in the world,
a noise as faint as that of a fly
walking on a windowpane.
He listened.
Then he recognized the sound
as that of snake scales
scratching on brickwork.
He knew immediately
that it was Nag or Nagaina
trying to enter the house.
But where?

He remembered a loose brick
at the back of the bathroom;
the brick could be pulled out
to drain the bath water
from the tub
to the creek near the house.
Plumbing facilities in India
are not always the same as ours.
Rikki-tikki crept
down the dark hall
and turned into the bathroom.

Pressing his lithe body
against the plastered wall,
he listened
and heard Nag and Nagaina
whispering together
outside in the moonlight.
Nag was saying,
"You go back to our nest
in the melon patch
at the back of the garden,
Nagaina.
Take care of our eggs.
They have been left alone too long.
I will creep into the bathroom
and wait
until the master comes in
for his bath in the morning.
Then I'll kill him
and his wife and his child.
When the family is dead,
the bungalow will be empty,
and Rikki-tikki will leave here.
And once again
the garden will belong to us.

Rikki-tikki heard
Nagaina slither off
toward the melon patch
at the back of the garden.

Then he saw,
or thought he saw,
the black beady eyes
of the cobra
as Nag pushed his head
around the loose brick
and pulled
the cold five feet of his body
into the room after him.
Rikki-tikki heard the cobra
rise up and lap water
from the water jar.
Then he heard the cobra
wrap himself, coil by coil,
around the bulge
at the bottom of the water jar.

After an hour
Rikki-tikki began to move,
muscle by muscle,
towards the jar.

Nag was asleep,
and Rikki-Tikki looked
at his big back, wondering
which would be the best place
for a good hold.
"If I don't break his back
at the first jump," said Rikki,
"he can still fight;
and if he fights — O Rikki!"

He looked at the thickness
of the neck below the hood,
but that was too much for him;
and a bite near the tail
would only make Nag savage.
"It must be the head,"
he said at last.
"The head above the hood;
and, when I am once there,
I must not let go."

Then he jumped
and sank his teeth deep
into Nag's head
which was lying a little clear
of the water jar.

It took Nag only a moment
to uncoil.
Then he battered Rikki-tikki
to and fro,
as a rat is shaken by a dog,
to and fro on the floor,
up and down,
and around in great circles.
Rikki-tikki thought
he would surely be killed
in the encounter,
but he was certain of one thing:
when the family found him,
he would still be clinging
to the snake's head.

Then Rikki-tikki saw
a ball of fire shoot past him,
and he felt its hot breath...
When he regained consciousness,
Teddy was holding
the little mongoose
in his arms,
showering him
with praise and affection.
He was saying that Rikki-tikki
had saved the family.
Teddy's father
had been awakened
by the fight in the bathroom,
and he had fired two shots
into the cobra's hood.
Nag, the black king cobra,
was dead.

Without waiting for breakfast,
Rikki-tikki escaped
to the veranda
and nursed his tired
and bruised body
in the warm sunshine.
He stretched out
on the brickwork
and was almost asleep
when he heard Darzee singing,
"Nag is dead — is dead —
is dead!"

Nag is killed in a battle with the little mongoose.

The news of Nag's death
was all over the garden,
and the frogs and birds joined
in the chorus, "Nag is dead —
is dead — is dead!"

"Yes," said Darzee.
"The maid has thrown
Nag's lifeless body
out on the rubbish heap.
Nag will never eat my babies
again."

"Oh, you stupid
tuft of feathers,"
said Rikki angrily.
"Is this the time to sing?
Where is Nagaina?"

"Nag is dead — is dead —
is dead!" Darzee went on,
singing at the top of her voice.
"The valiant Rikki-tikki
caught Nag by the head
and held fast.
The big man brought
the bang-stick,
and Nag fell in two pieces."

"Stop singing a minute, Darzee,"
said Rikki.
"Where is Nagaina?"

"What is it,
O Killer of the terrible Nag?"
asked Darzee.

"Where is Nagaina?"

"On the rubbish heap
by the stables,
mourning for Nag.
Great is Rikki-tikki
with the white teeth."

"Bother my white teeth!
Have you ever heard
where she keeps her eggs?"

"In the melon bed,
on the end nearest the wall,
where the sun strikes
nearly all day," said Darzee.
"She hid them there
three weeks ago."

Rikki-tikki turned
and flew down the garden path,
past the stable
and the tool shed,
on to the melon patch
near the wall.
There,
underneath the melon leaves,
he found Nagaina's nest
very cunningly concealed.
In it were twenty-six cobra eggs.

A cobra's nest
is nothing more than a hole
scooped out in the soft earth.
The cobra eggs
looked not unlike the eggs
that we keep in our refrigerator
at home,
except that the cobra eggs
were encased
in a soft, white, transparent skin
instead of in a hard shell.

Rikki-tikki finds Nagaina's nest in the garden.

Inside of each egg
Rikki-tikki could see
a baby cobra curled up,
and he knew
that the eggs would hatch
within the day.

The little mongoose
chuckled to himself
as he clipped the end
of the first egg
and killed the little snake
within it.
He remembered
that his mother had told him
that a baby cobra
can kill a man or a mongoose.

Methodically,
Rikki-tikki fished egg after egg
from the nest
and destroyed them.
All the while
he was keeping a sharp watch
lest Nagaina should return.
At last
there was but one egg left.

As Rikki-tikki pulled it
from the nest,
Darzee, the tailor-bird,
flew to him
from her nest in the pine tree,
screaming,
"Rikki-tikki!
Come! Come!
Nagaina has gone
onto the veranda!
Oh, come quickly!
She means killing!"

Rikki-tikki grasped the last egg
in his mouth
and scuttled up the garden path
as hard
as he could put foot to ground.
He bounded up the veranda steps
two at a time.

What he saw
caused him to stop so short
that he skidded
halfway across the brickwork.
Teddy, his father and mother
were seated there
at early breakfast,
but Rikki-tikki saw
that they were not eating.
They sat stone-still,
and their faces were white.

Coiled at the foot
of Teddy's chair
within easy striking distance
of Teddy's bare leg
was Nagaina.
She was swaying to and fro,
singing a song of triumph.

Rikki-tikki fights Nagaina on the veranda.

"Son of the big man
that killed Nag!"
she hissed.
"Wait a little.
Keep very still,
all you three!
If you move
I strike,
and if you do not move
I strike.
Oh, foolish people
who killed my Nag!"

Teddy's eyes
were fixed on his father,
and all his father could do
was to whisper,
"Sit still, Teddy.
You mustn't move.
Teddy, you mustn't move."

Rikki-tikki
bounded out onto the veranda
behind Nagaina
and spit the last egg
from his mouth.
"Turn around, Nagaina.
Turn and fight!
Look at the last of your eggs.
I found your nest in the melon
patch and destroyed all
of the eggs but this one."

Nagaina spun clear round,
forgetting everything
for the sake of her one egg.
At the same moment
Teddy's father
shot out a big hand,
caught Teddy by the shoulder,
and dragged him across the table,
spilling the dishes and the food
to the floor with a clatter.
"Tricked! Tricked! *Rikk-tck-tck!*"
chuckled Rikki-tikki.
"The boy is safe now,
and it was I — I — I
that caught Nag by the hood
last night in the bathroom."
The little mongoose began
to jump up and down,
all four feet together,
his head close to the floor.
"Nag threw me to and fro,
but he couldn't shake me off.
He was dead before the big man
blew him in two.
I did it!
Rikki-tikki-tck-tck!
Come, then, Nagaina.
Come and fight with me.
You shall not be a widow long."

Now the family drew back
against the porch railing,
watching the battle
of life and death
that was taking place
before them.
Nagaina was striking
again and again.
After each strike
she would recoil
as quickly as a watch-spring,
ready to strike again.
Rikki-tikki
was bounding all around Nagaina,
keeping just out of reach
of her stroke.
His little pink eyes
had turned red,
like hot coals.
He was standing up
on his hind feet
like a little kangaroo,
ready to spring
at the snake's neck
whenever he found the opening.
All the while
he was sounding his battle cry,
"*Rikki-tikki tck-tck!*"

Again and again and again
she struck.
Each time her head came
with a whack
on the brickwork of the veranda,
she gathered herself
together to strike again.

Rikki-tikki danced in a circle
to get behind her,
and Nagaina spun round
to keep her head to his head.

Rikki had forgotten the egg.
He had moved so far from it,
that Nagaina came nearer
and nearer to it.
At last, she caught the egg
in her mouth,
turned to the veranda steps,
and flew like an arrow
down the path —
with Rikki-tikki right behind.

It is said
that when the cobra
runs for its life,
it goes like the whiplash
flicked across the horse's neck.
But Rikki-tikki was even faster.
He caught Nagaina by the tail
as she plunged into the rat hole
where she and Nag used to live.
Rikki-tikki tried to pull her back,
but Nagaina was the stronger
of the two,
and inch by inch,
she pulled the little mongoose
into the hole with her.

And Darzee, the tailor-bird,
who was sitting in the pine tree
watching the battle
taking place below,
set up a very mournful chant:
"It's all over
with Rikki-tikki-tavi!
Brave Rikki-tikki-tavi!
Even a wise, full-grown mongoose
would not follow a cobra
into its own hole."

He stopped
to shake the dust
from his whiskers;
then he looked up at Darzee,
the tailor-bird,
and said:
"It's all over.
Nagaina is dead."

And the red ants that lived
between the grass stems
heard him
and began trooping down
one after another
to see
if what Rikki-tikki-tavi had said
was true.

Rikki's triumph is complete.

Presently
the grass
that grew around the rat hole
quivered,
and Rikki-tikki-tavi,
covered with dirt,
dragged himself out of the hole
leg by leg.

And as for Rikki-tikki-tavi,
he lay down in the sunshine
beside the rat hole
and went to sleep.
He slept all of that morning
and half of the afternoon,
because
for a little mongoose
he had done a hard day's work.

Here is a gallery of ten bird pictures, painted by the talented artist Basil Ede of Surrey, England. Many people think that Mr. Ede is the best painter of birds since Audubon made his prize collection of lifelike bird paintings in the early 1800's. Certainly Mr. Ede's pictures are lifelike, but he says that his aim is not to show his skill as a painter.

Birds in a Gallery

He wants people to see the character of each bird. That is why he paints them. It is impossible to look at these pictures without seeing the character of each bird, but it also is impossible to look at these paintings without knowing that you are having a rare experience. Just to see the beautiful coloring and shapes and movement makes you suddenly realize that you are alive, that the birds and artists and books and music contribute to the excitement of living.

Yellow-shafted Flicker ▶ has a strong bill for boring into tree bark for insects. His sharp claws hold him fast to the tree as he listens for insects under the bark. When something stirs, he attacks it.

Robin
is noted
for his red breast
and his cheery song
which begins at dawn.
Many people
consider the robin
the first sign
of spring.

Tree Swallow
might be nesting
in your birdhouse
in the backyard.
These birds
have strong wings.
They sometimes fly
10,000 miles
in a single year's
migration.

Belted Kingfisher
has been so busy fishing
it seems
that he hasn't had time
to preen his feathers.
Birds use their beaks
to dress their feathers
with oil which they take
from their bodies.

Black-capped Chickadee
is a gay
and active bird.
He darts about
in and out of trees
and open spaces,
calling his name,
"*Chickadee!
dee-dee-dee.*"

Pileated Woodpecker ➡

is a "woodworking machine." He has a powerful neck, a heavy skull, and a chisel-like bill for working his way into hollow trees. Notice how he balances himself with his tail and claws as he chops at the tree.

Hairy Woodpecker

looks almost like the downy woodpecker, except it is larger. Both of these woodpeckers are "bark-stickers" looking for insects.

⬆

Baltimore Oriole is one of the prettiest of birds. His clear, loud whistle in May and June announces that he is in the neighborhood once again to build a hanging nest in a high tree.

Eastern Evening Grosbeaks
travel in flocks varying from three to a
hundred. The plumes of the mother bird
are less colorful than those of the males,
which is true of many kinds of birds.

Grosbeaks

Great Horned Owl ➤
has eyes that collect light and ears that
collect sounds, making him the best
nighttime hunter of all birds. His feathers are so soft that they muffle the
sound as he swoops down on his prey.
Notice how his claws are shaped for
grasping.

choral reading

The teacher is speaking:
"This old rhyme by Alfred Noyes
is a favorite with boys and girls
because they seem to enjoy
seeing Daddy looking foolish.
I'll read it aloud first.
(The teacher does.)
Now you read it with me.
Ready? Here we go:

"Now, let's read it again,
but this time:

1) In the first verse,
   let your voices tell me
   that everyone is grumbling—
   until that happy moment
   when Daddy fell into the pond!

2) In the second verse,
   let your voices tell me
   that your faces are merry
   and bright.
   Let me hear the camera *click!*
   with a high crisp
   speaking of the word,
   or with that throat sound
   that you boys make so well, *tschk!*

3) In the third verse,
   let your voices tell me
   that the gardener
   is *laughing* silently
   so Daddy won't hear,
   and let me hear
   the sound of *quacking* ducks
   who also seem to know
   how to enjoy a catastrophe.

4) And when we come
   to the last three lines,
   let's have a pause
   after the word *respond,*
   then stretch out the word *when*
   like a rush of roaring wind,
   and then say,
   quickly and spritely,
   like the music coming up
   at the end of a funny TV show,
   Daddy fell into the pond!

"And now, let's read it again,
boys and girls,
taking the parts
as they are marked."

An essay by Bill Martin, Jr.

280

Daddy Fell into the Pond

Solo 1: Everyone grumbled. The sky was gray.
High voices: We had nothing to do and nothing to say.
Low voices: We were nearing the end of a dismal day,
Solo 2: And there seemed to be nothing beyond,
Teacher: THEN
All: *Daddy fell into the pond!*

Girls: And everyone's face grew merry and bright,
         And Timothy danced for sheer delight.
Boys: "Give me the camera, quick, oh quick!
         He's crawling out of the duckweed." *Click!*

Girls: Then the gardener suddenly slapped his knee,
         And doubled up, shaking silently,
Boys: And the ducks all quacked as if they were daft
Teacher: And it sounded as if the old drake laughed.

All: O, there wasn't a thing that didn't respond
                    WHEN
         Daddy fell into the pond!

A poem by Alfred Noyes

I Heard a Bird Sing

All: I heard a bird sing
     In the dark of December
A magical thing
     And sweet to remember.

Solo: "We are nearer to Spring
     Than we were in September,"
All: I heard a bird sing
     In the dark of December.

A poem by Oliver Herford,
picture by Tom O'Sullivan

The Pasture

All: I'm going out to clean the pasture spring;
I'll only stop to rake the leaves away
(And wait to watch the water clear, I may):
I shan't be gone long. —You come too.

I'm going out to fetch the little calf
That's standing by the mother. It's so young
It totters when she licks it with her tongue.
I shan't be gone long. —You come too.

A poem by Robert Frost

The Robin

The robin comes in spring
And fills the air with merry song,
And makes the fields and meadows ring,
Cheer-up!
Cheer-up!
O robin, sing,
Lift your voice,
The air is warm,
The flowers are born,
Sing...sing...sing...sing,
O lovely robin, *sing.*

A poem by Helen I. May

J's the Jumping Jay-Walker

Solo 1: J's the jumping Jay-walker,

Solo 2:　　A sort of human jeep.

Solo 3: He crosses where the lights are red.

Solo 4:　　Before he looks, he'll leap!

Girls: Then many a wheel

　　　　Begins to squeal,

Boys:　　And many a brake to slam.

All: He turns your knees to jelly

　　　And the traffic into jam.

A poem by Phyllis McGinley,
picture by Tom O'Sullivan

My Old 'Coon Dog

An American folk song,
with lyrics by Burl Ives

My old 'coon dog,
my old 'coon dog,
I wish you'd bring him back.
He chased the old sow
over the fence
And the little pig
through
the crack, crack, crack.
And the little pig
through the crack.

My old 'coon dog,
my old 'coon dog,
He chased a 'coon up a tree.
And when I shot
that racoon down,
It was twice as big
as me, me, me.
It was twice as big
as me.

Old Woman, Old Woman

Boys, moderately loud: Old woman, old woman, shall we go a-shearing?
Old woman, old woman, shall we go a-shearing?
Girls: Speak a little louder, sir, I'm very hard of hearing.

Boys, a bit louder: Old woman, old woman, are you good at spinning?
Old woman, old woman, are you good at spinning?
Girls: Speak a little louder, sir, I'm very hard of hearing.

Boys, louder: Old woman, old woman, can you darn my stockings?
Old woman, old woman, can you darn my stockings?
Girls: Speak a little louder, sir, I'm very hard of hearing.

Boys, whisper: Old woman, old woman, shall I love you dearly?
Old woman, old woman, shall I love you dearly?
Girls: Thank you very kindly, sir, I hear you very clearly!

Anonymous

My old 'coon dog,
my old 'coon dog,
He went to chase a 'coon;
He started the chase
at the first of March
And ended the tenth
of June, June, June.
And ended the tenth
of June.

My old 'coon dog,
my old 'coon dog,
He died one afternoon;
I woke with a fright
that very same night
And heard him chasing
a 'coon, 'coon, 'coon.
And heard him chasing
a 'coon.

My old 'coon dog,
my old 'coon dog,
I wish you'd bring him back.
He chased the old sow
over the fence
And the little pig
through
the crack, crack, crack.
And the little pig
through the crack.

There Was a Naughty Boy

There was a naughty boy,
    And a naughty boy was he,
He ran away to Scotland,
    The people there to see.

Then he found
That the ground
    Was as hard,
    That a yard
    Was as long,
    That a song
    Was as merry,
    That a cherry
    Was as red,
    That lead
Was as weighty,
    That fourscore
Was as eighty,
    That a door
Was as wooden
As in England—

So he stood in his shoes
    And he wondered,
        He wondered,
    He stood in his shoes
    And he wondered.

A poem by John Keats

The Snail

Little snail,
Dreaming you go.
Weather and rose
Is all you know.

Weather and rose
Is all you see.
Drinking
The dewdrop's
Mystery.

A poem by Langston Hughes

A Day

All: I'll tell you how the sun arose,—
　　A ribbon at a time.
　　The steeples swam in amethyst,
　　The news like squirrels ran.

　　The hills untied their bonnets,
　　The bobolinks began.
　　Then I said softly to myself,
　　"That must have been the sun!"

A poem by Emily Dickinson,
picture by Tom O'Sullivan

Weather

Boys: When the wind is in the east,
　　　'Tis neither good for man nor beast;
Girls: When the wind is in the north,
　　　The skillful fisher goes not forth;
Teacher: When the wind is in the south,
　　　It blows the bait in the fishes' mouth;
All: When the wind is in the west,
　　　Then 'tis at the very best.

Mother Goose

The Sniffle

In spite of her sniffle,
Isabel's chiffle.
Some girls with a sniffle
Would be weepy and tiffle;
They would look awful,
Like a rained-on waffle,
But Isabel's chiffle
In spite of her sniffle.
Her nose is more red
With a cold in her head,
But then, to be sure,
Her eyes are bluer.
Some girls with a snuffle,
Their tempers are uffle,
But when Isabel's snivelly
She's snivelly civilly,
And when she is snuffly
She's perfectly luffly.

A poem by Ogden Nash

The Fairies

Up the airy mountain,
    Down the rushy glen,
We daren't go a-hunting,
    For fear of little men;
Wee folk, good folk,
    Trooping all together;
Green jacket, red cap,
    And white owl's feather!

Down along the rocky shore
    Some make their home,
They live on crispy pancakes
    Of yellow tide-foam;
Some in the reeds
    Of the black mountain-lake,
With frogs for their watchdogs,
    All night awake.

A poem by William Allingham

Here is a poem for solo and group reading. Why not divide into small groups and figure out your own choral arrangements?

Song
of the Train

**A poem by David McCord,
picture by Tom O'Sullivan**

(Softly)   Clickety-clack,
Wheels on the track,
This is the way
They begin the attack:
(Louder)   Click-ety-clack,
Click-ety-clack.
Click-ety, clack-ety,
Click-ety,
Clack.

(Louder)   Clickety-clack,
Over the crack,
Faster and faster
The song of the track:
Clickety-clack,
Clickety-clack,
Clickety, clackety,
Clackety,
Clack.

(Softly)   Riding in front,
Riding in back,
Everyone hears
The song of the track:
*(Very
softly)*   Clickety-clack,
Clickety-clack,
Clickety, clickety,
Clackety,
Clack.

Jonathan Bing

All: Poor old Jonathan Bing
Went out in his carriage to visit the King,
Girls: But everyone pointed and said, 'Look at that!
Jonathan Bing has forgotten his hat!'
Boys: (He'd forgotten his hat!)

All: Poor old Jonathan Bing
Went home and put on a new hat for the King,
Boys: But by the palace a soldier said, 'Hi!
You can't see the King; you've forgotten your tie!'
Girls: (He'd forgotten his tie!)

All: Poor old Jonathan Bing
He put on a beautiful tie for the King,
High voices: But when he arrived, an Archbishop said, 'Ho!
You can't come to court in pajamas, you know!'
Low voices: (He'd come in pajamas!)

All: Poor old Jonathan Bing
Went home and addressed a short note to the King:
'If you please will excuse me, I won't come to tea;
For home's the best place for all people like me!'

A poem by Beatrice Curtis Brown

The Hunter

The hunter crouches in his blind
'Neath camouflage of every kind,
And conjures up a quacking noise
To lend allure to his decoys.
This grown-up man, with pluck and luck,
Is hoping to outwit a duck.

A poem by Ogden Nash

I Sometimes Think

High voices: I sometimes think I'd rather crow
And be a rooster than to roost
And be a crow. But I dunno.

Middle voices: A rooster he can roost also,
Which don't seem fair when crows can't crow.
Which may help some. Still I dunno.

Low voices: Crows should be glad of one thing, though,
Nobody thinks of eating crow,
While roosters they are good enough
For anyone unless they're tough.

All: There are lots of tough old roosters though,
And anyway a crow can't crow,
So mebby roosters stand more show.
It looks that way. But I dunno.

Anonymous,
picture by Tom O'Sullivan

291

LITTLE CHARLIE CHIPMUNK
HE CHATTERED
AND HE CHATTERED
HE CHATTERED
AND HE CHATTERED
HE CHATTERED
AND HE CHATTERED
HE CHATTERED

OH,

WAS A TALKER, MERCY ME!
AFTER BREAKFAST
AFTER TEA!
TO HIS FATHER
TO HIS MOTHER!
TO HIS SISTER
TO HIS BROTHER!
TILL HIS FAMILY WAS ALMOST
 DRIVEN WILD.
LITTLE CHARLIE CHIPMUNK
 WAS A VERY TIRESOME
CHILD!

A poem by Helen Cowles LeCron

A story by Carl Sandburg,
drawings by David Czarin

294

The Huckabuck Family

and how they raised corn.

Jonas Jonas Huckabuck was a farmer in Nebraska
with a wife, Mama Mama Huckabuck,
and a daughter, Pony Pony Huckabuck.

"Your father gave you two names the same in front,"
people had said to him.

And he answered, "Yes, two names are easier to remember.
If you call me by my first name Jonas
and I don't hear you,
then when you call me by my second name Jonas
maybe I will."

"And," he went on,
"I call my pony-face girl Pony Pony
because if she doesn't hear me the first time
she always does the second."

And so they lived on a farm where they raised popcorn,
these three,
Jonas Jonas Huckabuck,
and his wife, Mama Mama Huckabuck,
and their pony-face daughter, Pony Pony Huckabuck.

After they harvested
   the crop one year,
they had the barns,
the cribs, the sheds, the shacks,
   and all the cracks
and corners of the farm,
all filled with popcorn.

"We came out to Nebraska
to raise popcorn,"
   said Jonas Jonas,
"and I guess
we got nearly enough popcorn
this year
for the popcorn poppers
and all the friends
   and relations
of all the popcorn poppers
in these United States."

And this was the year
that Pony Pony was going
   to bake her first squash pie
all by herself.
In one corner of the corncrib,
all covered over with popcorn,
she had a secret,
a big round squash,
a fat yellow squash,
a rich squash
all spotted with spots of gold.

She carried the squash
into the kitchen,
took a long sharp shining knife,
and then she cut the squash
in the middle
till she had two big half squashes.
And inside
just like the outside
it was rich yellow
spotted with spots of gold.

And there was a shine of silver.
And Pony Pony wondered
why silver should be in a squash.
She picked and plunged
with her fingers
till she pulled it out.

"It's a buckle," she said,
"a silver buckle,
  a Chinese silver slipper buckle."
  She ran with it
  to her father
  and said,
"Look what I found
  when I cut open
  the golden yellow squash
  spotted with gold spots—
  it is a Chinese
  silver slipper buckle."

"It means our luck
  is going to change,
  and we don't know
  whether it will be good luck
  or bad luck,"
    said Jonas Jonas
  to his daughter
  Pony Pony Huckabuck.

Then she ran with it to her mother
    and said,
"Look what I found
  when I cut open the yellow squash
  spotted with spots of gold—
  it is a Chinese
  silver slipper buckle."

"It means our luck
  is going to change,
  and we don't know
  whether it will be
  good luck or bad luck,"
    said Mama Mama Huckabuck.

And that night...

...a fire started

in the barns, cribs, sheds,
shacks, cracks, and corners
where the popcorn harvest
   was kept.

All night long
the popcorn popped.
In the morning
the ground all around
the farm house and the barn
was covered with white popcorn,
so it looked like
a heavy fall of snow.

All the next day

the fire kept on
and the popcorn popped
till it was up to the shoulders
of Pony Pony
when she tried to walk
from the house to the barn.
And that night
in all the barns, cribs, sheds,
shacks, cracks, and corners
of the farm,
the popcorn went on popping.

In the morning

when Jonas Jonas Huckabuck
looked out of the upstairs window,
he saw the popcorn popping
and coming higher and higher.
It was nearly up to the window.
Before evening and dark
of that day,
Jonas Jonas Huckabuck
and his wife Mama Mama Huckabuck
and their daughter
Pony Pony Huckabuck,
all went away from the farm
   saying,
"We came to Nebraska
to raise popcorn,
but this is too much.
We will not come back
till the wind blows away
the popcorn.
We will not come back
till we get a sign and a signal."

And the next year

they went to Oskaloosa, Iowa.
Pony Pony Huckabuck
   was very proud
because when she stood
on the sidewalks in the street,
she could see her father
sitting high on the seat
of a coal wagon,
driving two big spanking horses
hitched with shining brass harness
in front of the coal wagon.
And though Pony Pony
and Jonas Jonas were proud,
very proud all that year,
there never came a sign, a signal.

The next year again

was a proud year,
exactly as proud a year
as they spent in Oskaloosa.
They went to Paducah, Kentucky;
to Defiance, Ohio;
Peoria, Illinois;
Indianapolis, Indiana;
Walla Walla, Washington.
And in all these places
Pony Pony Huckabuck
saw her father,
Jonas Jonas Huckabuck,
standing in rubber boots
deep down in a ditch
with a shining steel shovel

shoveling yellow clay
and black mud
from down in the ditch
high and high
up over his shoulders.
And though it was a proud year,
they got no sign, no signal.

The next year came.

It was the proudest of all.
This was the year
Jonas Jonas Huckabuck
and his family
lived in Elgin, Illinois,
and Jonas Jonas was watchman
in a watch factory
watching the watches.

"I know where you have been,"
Mama Mama Huckabuck would say
of an evening
to Pony Pony Huckabuck.
"You have been down
to the watch factory
watching your father
watch the watches."

"Yes," said Pony Pony.
"Yes, and this evening
when I was watching father
watch the watches
in the watch factory,
I looked over my left shoulder
and I saw a policeman
with a star and brass buttons,
and he was watching me
to see if I was watching father
watch the watches
in the watch factory."

It was a proud year.
Pony Pony saved her money.
Thanksgiving came.
Pony Pony said,
"I am going to get a squash
to make a squash pie."
She hunted from one grocery
to another;
she kept her eyes
on the farm wagons
coming into Elgin
with squashes.

She found what she wanted,
the yellow squash
spotted with gold spots.

She took it home,
cut it open,
and saw the inside
was like the outside,
all rich yellow
spotted with gold spots.

There was a shine like silver.
She picked and plunged
with her fingers
and pulled and pulled
till at last she pulled out
the shine of silver.

"It's a sign!
It is a signal," she said.
"It is a buckle,
a silver buckle,
a Chinese silver slipper buckle.
It is the mate to the other buckle.
Our luck is going to change.
Yoo hoo! Yoo hoo!"

She told her father and mother
about the buckle.
They went back to the farm
in Nebraska.
The wind by this time
had been blowing and blowing
for three years,
and all the popcorn
was blown away.

"Now we are going
to be farmers again,"
said Jonas Jonas Huckabuck
to Mama Mama Huckabuck
and to Pony Pony Huckabuck.
"And we are going to raise
cabbages, beets, and turnips;
we are going to raise
squash, rutabaga, pumpkins,
and peppers for pickling.
We are going to raise
wheat, oats, barley, rye.
We are going to raise
corn such as Indian corn
and kaffir corn —
but we are not going to raise
any popcorn
for the popcorn poppers
to be popping."

And the pony-face daughter,
Pony Pony Huckabuck,
was proud because
she had on new black slippers,
and around her ankles,
holding the slippers
on the left foot
and the right foot,
she had two buckles,
silver buckles,
Chinese silver slipper buckles.
They were mates.

Sometimes
on Thanksgiving Day
and Christmas
and New Year's,
she tells her friends
to be careful
when they open a squash.

"Squashes make your luck change
good to bad
and bad to good,"
says Pony Pony.

creative
dramatics

An essay by Bill Martin, Jr.

Most everybody likes a play.
Most everybody likes to be in a play.
In this section of *Sounds of Mystery*, we have included a poem,
a chanting game, and a story that are really fun to act out.
Don't make the mistake of thinking
that a play has to be a grand performance
with perfect scenery and costumes—
although this can be fun, too.
You probably remember times out of school
when two or three people or the whole neighborhood
made a play without the slightest suggestion of a costume
or scenery. This is a good way to begin creative dramatics
in your classroom. As a starter, several of you may get up
in front of the class and act out the poem "Jonathan Bing"
while it is being read aloud by the rest of the class (page 290).
Later, several of you may want to act out "Jonathan Bing"
making up your own speeches as you go along.
After acting it out once, you may want to choose another group
of boys and girls to do the same thing,
making up their own speeches as they wish.

You will find the two plays are both alike yet different.
The play can grow and grow, until, finally,
everyone will have a part.
Some can be people watching the King pass by,
some can be footmen attending the King,
some can be the horses drawing the King's coach.
One can be the soldier, one can be the Archbishop,
and, of course, you'll need the King and Jonathan Bing.
You may have exciting ideas of how to make
just a hint of a costume for each character,
such as a crown for the King,
using materials that you have in the classroom.
And when the play takes shape,
what fun you'll have inviting other classes in to see it.

"Overheard on a Saltmarsh" is a dramatic poem or dialogue
that can be acted out "with voices only" like a choral reading,
the boys reading the goblin's lines,
and the girls reading the nymph's lines.
However, if you want to make it into a spooky play
with actual characters and perhaps a verse-speaking chorus
of waving weeds, and maybe an owl that wings in
over the marsh from time to time, here is your chance.

"I'll Give to You a Paper of Pins" is a chanting game
in which the boys chorus one part, and the girls respond.
You may want to use simple dance steps in acting out this game,
because this is how singing and chanting games began.

The boys may march forward, for example, while saying,
"O miss, I'll give you a paper of pins," and
the girls can swish around in back of them
when they reply that they're not interested.
You can add your own ideas, using any
of the modern or old-time dance steps that you enjoy.
The last selection is "How Boots Befooled the King."
Now here is a story worth making into a real play.
Everyone should have a part. You can add balloon sellers,
people going to market, a court full of fair ladies
and fine lords, and as many other characters as you wish.
If someone in your class strongly prefers to be "backstage"
holding up the scenery or opening and closing the curtains,
this also is being "in" the play.
You may begin by finding the episodes in the story
and acting them out, one by one.
Finally, you can put all of the episodes together
for a longer and richer dramatic experience.

I recommend that you don't write down speeches
or try to memorize lines from the story.
Just get to know your character well enough
so that you can make up the speeches as you go along.
You'll find the speeches flowing,
and you'll never need to worry about forgetting
what you want to say.
"How Boots Befooled the King" also would make
a wonderful puppet show—another form of creative dramatics.

A Storytelling Picture for Acting Out ▶
by Trina Schart Hyman

Enjoy the dramatic poem as a choral reading, with the boys intoning the goblin's mysterious questions (in black) and the girls responding eerily for the nymph (in white).

Overheard on a Saltmarsh

NYMPH, NYMPH, WHAT ARE YOUR BEADS?

Green glass, goblin. Why do you stare at them?

GIVE THEM ME.

NO

GIVE THEM ME...

GIVE THEM ME.

NO

THEN I WILL HOWL ALL NIGHT IN THE
REEDS, LIE IN THE MUD AND
HOWL FOR THEM

Goblin, why do you love them so?

THEY ARE BETTER THAN STARS OR WATER,
BETTER THAN VOICES OF WINDS THAT SING,
BETTER THAN ANY MAN'S FAIR
DAUGHTER, YOUR GREEN
GLASS BEADS ON A
SILVER STRING.

Hush, I stole them out of the moon.

GIVE ME YOUR BEADS, I WANT THEM.

NO.

I WILL HOWL IN A DEEP LAGOON
FOR YOUR GREEN GLASS BEADS,
I LOVE THEM SO.
GIVE THEM ME. GIVE THEM.

NO.

A dramatic dialogue by Harold Monro,
illustrated by Eric Carle

I'll Give to You a Paper of Pins

This chanting game gives the girls a chance to turn up their noses and toss their heads to the earnest pleas of the boys to marry; but in the end, it is the boys who turn thumbs down and remain bachelors.

Boys:

"O miss, I'll give you a paper of pins,
If you will tell me how love begins:
    If you will marry, marry, marry,
    If you will marry me."

Girls:

"I'll not accept your paper of pins,
And I won't tell you how love begins;
    For I won't marry, marry, marry,
    For I won't marry you."

"O miss, I'll give you a coach and six,
Every horse as black as pitch.
    If you will marry, marry, marry,
    If you will marry me."

"I'll not accept, *etc.*"

"O miss, I'll give you a red silk gown,
With gold and laces hanging round.
    If you will marry, marry, marry,
    If you will marry me."

"I'll not accept, *etc.*"

"O miss, I'll give you a little gold bell,
To ring for the waiter when you are not well.
    If you will marry, marry, marry,
    If you will marry me."

                  "I'll not accept, *etc.*"

"O miss, I'll give you the key to my heart,
That we may lock and never part.
    If you will marry, marry, marry,
    If you will marry me."

                  "I'll not accept, *etc.*"

"O miss, I'll give you the key to my chest,
That you may have money at your request.
    If you will marry, marry, marry,
    If you will marry me."

            "I will accept the key of your chest,
              That I may have money at my request.
                  For I will marry, marry, marry,
                  For I will marry you."

"Ah, I see, money is all,
Woman's love is none at all;
    For I won't marry, marry, marry,
    For I won't marry you."

Anonymous

ONCE upon a time there was a king who was the wisest in all of the world. So wise was he that no one had ever befooled him, which is a rare thing, I can tell you.

Now, this king had a daughter who was as pretty as a ripe apple, so that there was no end to the number of the lads who came asking to marry her. Every day there were two or three of them dawdling around the house, so that at last the old king grew tired of having them always about.

HOW BOOTS BEFOOLED THE KING

An Irish folktale
retold by Ruth Sawyer,
linoleum cuts by Eric Carle

So he sent word far and near
that whoever should befool him
might have the princess
and half of the kingdom to boot,
for he thought that it would be
a wise man indeed
who could trick him.

But the king also said
that whoever should try
to befool him and should fail
should have a good whipping.
This was to keep
all foolish fellows away.
But the princess was so pretty
that there was no lack of lads
who came to have a try
for her and half of the kingdom,
but every one of these went away
with a sore back and no luck.

Now, there was a man
who was well off in the world,
and who had three sons;
the first was named Peter,
and the second was named Paul.
Peter and Paul thought themselves
as wise as anybody
in all of the world,
and their father thought
as they did.
As for the youngest son,
he was named Boots.
Nobody thought anything of him
except that he was silly,
for he did nothing but sit
poking warm ashes all of the day.

One morning Peter spoke up
and said that he was going
to the town
to have a try
at befooling the king,
for it would be a fine thing
to have a princess
in the family.

His father did not say *no*,
for if anybody was wise enough
to befool the king,
Peter was the lad.

So, after Peter had eaten
a good breakfast,
off he set for the town,
right foot foremost.
After a while
he came to the king's house
and—*rap! tap! tap!*—
he knocked at the door.
Well, what did he want?
Oh! he would only like
to have a try
at befooling the king.
Very good;
he should have his try.
He was not the first one
who had been there that morning,
early as it was.
So Peter was shown in
to the king.

315

"Oh, look!" said he,
"yonder are three black geese
out in the courtyard!"

But no,
the king was not to be fooled
so easily as all that.
"One goose is enough
to look at at a time," said he;
"take him away
and give him a whipping!"
And so they did,
and Peter went home
bleating like a sheep.

One day Paul spoke up.
"I should like to go
and have a try
for the princess, too," said he.

Well,
his father did not say *no*,
for, after all,
Paul was the more clever of the two.
So off Paul went
as merrily as a duck
in the rain.

By and by he came to the castle,
and then he, too,
was brought before the king
just as Peter had been.

"Oh, look!" said he,
"yonder is a crow
sitting in the tree
with three white stripes
on his back!"

But the king was not so silly
as to be fooled in that way.
"Here is a Jack," said he,
"who will soon have more stripes
on his back
than he will like;
take him away
and give him his whipping!"
Then it was done
as the king had said,
and Paul went away home
bawling like a calf.

One day up spoke Boots.
"I should like to go
and have a try
for the pretty princess, too,
said he.

At this

they all stared and sniggered.
What! He go
where his clever brothers
had failed,
and had nothing to show
for the trying
but a good beating?
What had come over the lout!
Here was a pretty business,
to be sure!
That was what they all said.

But all of this
rolled away from Boots
like water from a duck's back.

No matter,
he would like to go
and have a try
like the others.
So he begged and begged
until his father was glad
to let him go
to be rid of his teasing,
if nothing else.
Then Boots asked
if he might have
the old tattered hat
that hung back of the chimney.

Oh, yes
he might have that
if he wanted it,
for nobody with good wits
was likely to wear such a thing.
So Boots took the hat,
and after he had brushed the ashes
from his shoes,
set off for the town,
whistling as he went.

The first body whom he met
was an old woman
with a great load
of earthenware pots and crocks
on her shoulders.

"Good-day, mother," said Boots.

"Good-day, son," said she.

"What will you take
  for all of your pots and crocks?"
said Boots.

"Three shillings," said she.

"I will give you five shillings
  if you will come and stand
  in front of the king's house,
  and do thus and so
  when I say this and that,"
said Boots.

Oh, yes!
She would do that
willingly enough.

So Boots and the old woman
went on together,
and presently came
to the king's house.
When they had come there,
Boots sat down
in front of the door
and began bawling as loud as he could—
"No, I will not!
I will not do it, I say!
No, I will not do it!"

So he kept on,
bawling louder and louder
until he made such a noise
that, at last,
the king himself came out
to see what all the hubbub was about.
But when Boots saw him,
he only bawled out louder than ever.

"No, I will not!
I will not do it, I say!"

"Stop! Stop!" cried the king,
"What is all this about?"

"Why," said Boots,
"everybody wants to buy my cap,
but I will not sell it!

I will not do it, I say!"

"But why should anybody
want to buy
such a cap as that?" said the king

"Because," said Boots,
"it is a fooling cap
and the only one
in all of the world."

"A fooling cap!" said the king,
for he did not like to hear
of such a cap as that
coming into the town.
"Hum-m-m-m!
I should like to see you
fool somebody with it.
Could you fool
that old body yonder
with the pots and the crocks?"

"Oh yes!
That is easily enough done,"
said Boots, and without more ado
he took off his tattered cap
and blew into it.
Then he put it on his head again
and bawled out,
"Break pots! Break pots!"

No sooner had he spoken these words
than the old woman jumped up
and began breaking and smashing
her pots and crocks
as though she had gone crazy.
(That was what Boots
had paid her five shillings
for doing,
but of it the king knew nothing.)

"Hui!" said he to himself,
"I must buy that hat
from the fellow
or he will fool the princess
away from me for sure and certain."

Then he began talking to Boots
as sweetly as though
he had honey in his mouth.
*Perhaps Boots would sell
the hat to him?*

*Oh, no!
Boots could not think of
such a thing
as selling his fooling cap.*

*Come, come;
the king wanted that hat,
and sooner than miss buying it,
he would give
a whole bag of gold money for it.*

At this Boots looked up
and looked down,
scratching his head.
*Well, he supposed he would have
to sell the hat some time,
and the king
might as well have it
as anybody else.
But for all that
he did not like parting with it.*

So the king gave Boots
the bag of gold,
and Boots gave the king
the old tattered hat,
and then he went his way.

320

After Boots had gone,
the king blew into the hat
and blew into the hat,
but though he blew enough
breath into it
to sail a big ship,
he did not befool
so much as a single titmouse.
Then, at last, he began to see
that the fooling cap was good
on nobody else's head
but Boots';
and he was none too pleased at that,
you may be sure.

As for Boots,
with his bag of gold
he bought the finest clothes
that were to be had in the town,
and when the next morning had come,
he started away
bright and early
for the king's house.

"I have come," said he,
"to marry the princess,
if you please."

At this
the king hemmed and hawed
and scratched his head.
Yes, Boots had befooled him
sure enough,
but, after all,
he could not give up the princess
for such a thing as that.
Still,
he would give Boots
another chance.
Now there was the high-councillor,
who was the wisest man
in all of the world.
Did Boots think
that he could fool him also?

Oh, yes!
Boots thought
that it might be done.

Very well;
if he could befool the high-councillor
so as to bring him
to the castle
the next morning
against his will,
Boots should have the princess
and the half of the kingdom;
if he did not do so,
he should have his beating.

Then Boots went away
and the king thought
that he was rid of him now
for good and all.

As for the high-councillor,
he was not pleased
with the matter at all,
for he did not like the thought
of being fooled
by a clever rogue,
and taken here and there
against his will.

So when he had come home,
he armed all of his servants
with blunderbusses,
and then waited
to give Boots a *welcome*
when he should come.

But Boots was not going to fall
into any such trap as that!
No indeed! Not he!

The next morning he went quietly
and bought a fine large meal-sack.
Then he put a wig
over his beautiful hair,
so that no one might know him.

After that
he went to the place
where the high-councillor lived,
and when he had come there,
he crawled inside of the sack
and lay just beside
the door of the house.
By and by,
came one of the maid servants
to the door,
and there lay
the great meal-sack
with somebody in it.

"Ach!" cried she,
"who is there?"

But Boots only said, "Sh-h-h-h!"

Then the serving maid
went back into the house
and told the high-councillor

that one lay outside
in a great meal-sack
and that all that he said was,
"Sh-h-h-h-h."
So the councillor went himself
to see what it was all about.

"What do you want here?" said he.

"Sh-h-h-h-h!" said Boots,
"I am not to be talked to now.
This is a wisdom-sack,
and I am learning wisdom
as fast as a drake
can eat peas."

"And what wisdom have you learned?"
said the councillor.

Oh! Boots had learned wisdom
about everything in the world.
He had learned

that the clever scamp
who had fooled the king yesterday
was coming
with seventeen tall men
to take the high-councillor,
willy-nilly,
to the castle that morning.

When the high-councillor
heard this,
he fell to trembling
till his teeth rattled
in his head.

"And have you learned
how I can get the better
of this clever scamp?"
said he.

Oh, yes!
Boots had learned that
easily enough.

So, good!
Then if the wise man in the sack
would tell the high-councillor
how to escape the clever rogue,
the high-councillor
would give the wise man
twenty shillings.

But no,
that was not to be done;
wisdom was not bought so cheaply
as the high-councillor
seemed to think.

Well,
the councillor would give him
a hundred shillings, then.
That was good!
A hundred shillings
was a hundred shillings.
If the councillor

would give him that much,
he might get into the sack
              himself,
and then he could learn
all the wisdom that he wanted,
and more besides.

So Boots crawled out of the sack,
and the councillor
paid his hundred shillings
and crawled in.
As soon as he was in
all snug and safe,
Boots drew
the mouth of the sack together
and tied it tightly.
Then he flung sack,
councillor and all,
over his shoulder
and started away to the king's house,
and anybody who met them
could see with half an eye
that the councillor was going
against his will.

When Boots came
to the king's castle,
he laid the councillor down
in the goose-house,
and then he went to the king.

When the king saw Boots again,
he bit his lips
with vexation.

"Well," said he,
"have you fooled the councillor?"

"Oh, yes!" says Boots,
"I have done that."

And where was the councillor now?

Oh, Boots had just left him
down in the goose-house.
He was tied up
safe and sound
in a sack,
waiting

till the king
should send for him.

So the councillor was sent for,
and when he came,
the king saw at once
that he had been brought
against his will.

"And now
may I marry the princess?"
said Boots.

But the king was not willing
for him to marry the princess yet;
no! no!

Boots must not go so fast.
There was more to be done yet.
If he would come
tomorrow morning,
he might have the princess
and welcome,
but he would have to pick her out
from among fourscore other maids
just like her;
did he think
that he could do that?

Oh, yes!
Boots thought
that might be easy enough to do.

So, good!
Then come tomorrow;
but he must understand
that if he failed,
he should have a good whipping
and be sent packing
from the town.

So off went Boots,
and the king thought
that he was rid of him now,
for he had never seen the princess,
and how could he pick her out
from eighty others?

But Boots was not going
to give up so easily
as all that!

No, not he!
He made a little box,
and then he hunted up and down
until he had caught a live mouse
to put into it.

When the next morning came,
he started away
to the king's house,
taking his mouse along with him
in the box.
There was the king,
standing in the doorway,
looking out into the street.
When he saw Boots
coming towards him,
he made a wry face.

"What!" said he,
"are you back again?"

Oh, yes!
Boots was back again.
And now
if the princess was ready,
he would like
to go and find her,
for lost time
was not to be gathered again
like fallen apples.

So off they marched
to a great room,
and there stood
eighty-and-one maidens,
all as much alike
as peas in the same dish.
Boots looked here and there,
but even if he had known
the princess,
he could not have told her
from the others.
But he was ready
for all that.
Before anyone knew
what he was about,
he opened the box,
and out ran the little mouse
among them all.
Then what a screaming
and a hubbub
there was.
Many looked as though
they would have liked to swoon,
but only one of them did so.

As soon as the others
saw what had happened,

they forgot all about the mouse
and ran to her
and fell to fanning her
and slapping her hands
and chafing her temples.

"This is the princess,"
said Boots.

And so it was.

After that
the king could think
of nothing more
to set Boots to do,
so he let him
marry the princess
as he had promised
and have half of the kingdom
to boot.

That is all
of this story.
Only this:
It is not always
the silliest one
that sits kicking his feet
in the ashes at home.

If N**O**NE Ever Marries Me

If no one ever marries me—
    And I don't see why they should,
For they say I'm not pretty,
    And I'm seldom very good—

If no one ever marries me
    I shan't mind very much,
I shall buy a squirrel in a cage
    And a little rabbit-hutch;

I shall have a cottage near a wood,
    And a pony all my own,
And a little lamb, quite clean and tame,
    That I can take to town.

And when I'm getting really old—
    At twenty-eight or nine—
I shall find a little orphan-girl
    And bring her up as mine.

A poem by Laurence Alma-Tadema

The language that you use is pretty much your own choice.
It's one way of behaving so that other people can know
who you are. You may say, for example,

> *Your telephone call really threw me.*
> or *Your telephone call confused me but good.*
> or *Your telephone call baffled me.*
> or *Your telephone call befooled me.*

Which of these expressions would you choose to use
if the caller was your friend? your teacher? a stranger?
What does each of these expressions tell the other person
about you?

This kind of questioning will lead you to ask questions
about the way our language works. For example,
why is it in our language we say the *big red barn*
and the *pretty Italian girl*, but not the *red big barn*
and the *Italian pretty girl?*
Why is it that we have no difficulty in understanding
the different meanings of an expression, such as *looked up:*

> *Erin looked up from his work to say hello.*
> *Eric looked up the word in the big dictionary.*
> *Erika always looked up to her brother as if he were a hero.*

Why is it that the combination of letters *s-t-o-r-y*
is pronounced differently in each of these cases:

> *That was quite a **story**, Peter.*
> *You tell it as if it were his**tory**.*

Why is it that each of these expressions
mean approximately the same thing
even though the words change:

> *I'll be home about 5 o'clock.*
> *I'll be home at about 5 o'clock.*
> *I'll be home near 5 o'clock.*
> *I'll be home around 5 o'clock.*
> *I'll be home close to 5.*
> *I'm shooting to be home at 5 o'clock.*
> *My target for getting home is 5 o'clock.*

Isn't it interesting that our language permits certain words
to hop around within a sentence
without changing the meaning of the sentence?

> *She ran quickly.*
> *Quickly she ran.*
> *She quickly ran.*

Here's another miracle of our language.
The same word can actually change what it does
in a sentence. In one sentence it may name something.
In another, it may show what someone is doing.
In another sentence it may describe something.

> *A cross is a mark made by putting one line across another.*
> *"Cross out the mistakes on that page."*
> *Mrs. Alsop is always cross and grumpy when she is tired.*
>> —from *Word Wonder Dictionary*

So here you are, making choices again.
This time, choices about language.
Have you ever made the habit of keeping a list
of words that fascinate you?
Not the words that someone asks you to study or to memorize,
and not necessarily the words that you will find
in vocabulary tests, but just words that appeal to you.
Here is a beginning list from *Sounds of Mystery.*

> *You're really an ogre at heart.*
> *He came striding in like Giant Thunder.*
> *Let's sing that sweeten gooden song again.*
> *Oh, you're just a mental wizard!*
> *Thank you for your generous applause.*

As wet as a [fish] — as dry as a bone;

As live as a bird — as dead as a stone;

As plump as a partridge — as poor as a rat;

As strong as a [horse] — as weak as a [cat];

As hard as a flint — as soft as a mole;

As white as a lily — as black as a coal;

As plain as a staff — as rough as a [bear];

As tight as a [drum] — as free as the air;

As heavy as lead — as light as a [feather];

As steady as time — as uncertain as weather;

As hot as an oven — as cold as a [frog];

As gay as a lark — as sick as a [dog];

As savage as tigers — as mild as a dove;

As stiff as a poker — as limp as a [glove];

As blind as a bat — as deaf as a post;

As cool as a [cucumber] — as warm as toast;

As blunt as a [hammer] — as sharp as an awl;

As flat as a flounder — as round as a [ball];

As brittle as glass — as tough as gristle;

As neat as a pin — as clean as a [whistle];

As red as a [rose] — as square as a box;

As bold as a thief — as sly as a [fox].

Anonymous   pictures by Betty Fraser

SWINGING
on a star

A song by Johnny Burke

Would you like to swing on a star,
Carry moonbeams home in a jar,
And be better off than you are,
Or would you rather be a mule?

A mule is an animal with long funny ears,
He kicks up at anything he hears,
His back is brawny
And his brain is weak,
He's just plain stupid
With a stubborn streak,
And by the way if you hate to go to school,
You may grow up to be a mule.
Or would you like to swing on a star,
Carry moonbeams home in a jar,
And be better off than you are,
Or would you rather be a pig?

A pig is an animal with dirt on his face,
His shoes are a terrible disgrace,
He's got no manners
When he eats his food,
He's fat and lazy
And extremely rude,
But if you don't care a feather or a fig,
You may grow up to be a pig.
Or would you like to swing on a star,
Carry moonbeams home in a jar,
And be better off than you are,
Or would you rather be a fish?

A fish won't do anything but swim in a brook,
He can't write his name or read a book,
To fool the people
Is his only thought,
And though he's slippery,
He still gets caught,
But then if that sort of life is what you wish,
You may grow up to be a fish.

And all the monkeys aren't in the zoo,
Ev'ry day you meet quite a few,
So you see it's all up to you.
You can be better than you are,
You could be SWINGING
on a star.

Aloha

Hawaii, paradise islands.
Green-robed mountains
towering over the land,
rich fields of sugar cane
and pineapples
dotting the landscape,
a friendly sun brightening
the day after a rain,
stretching beaches of white sand
that welcome in the blue sea,
friendly people of many races
mixing their lives and languages
and dreams
in beautiful Hawaii.
Most family names in Hawaii
are Oriental names
like Chan, Okum, Yank
and Fujita,
because many immigrants
came years ago to Hawaii
from China, Japan and Korea
to work in the sugar cane
and pineapple fields.
Many workers also came
from the Philippine Islands,
Portugal and other places.
Consequently,
many different languages
and combinations of languages
are now spoken in Hawaii.

An editorial feature with water color by John Pike

Hawaiian Vowel	As in English
a	*ah*
e	*gay*
i	*see*
o	*oh*
u	sh*oot*

The seven consonants, *h, k, l, m, n, p, w*, are pronounced just as they are in English with one exception. When *w* is the next to the last letter in a word, it is sounded like *v*. *Hawi* is pronounced hah′ vee. When *e* is the last letter in a word, it is sometimes pronounced to rhyme with *see*. *Wahine* (woman) is pronounced wah hee′ nee, but *kane* (man) is pronounced kah′ nay.

The accent in a Hawaiian word is almost always on the next to last syllable.

The Hawaiian language
is written with only five vowels
and seven consonants.
The vowels and consonants
always signal the same sounds,
with the two exceptions
shown in the chart above.
Because the language
is so easy to pronounce,
you may want to learn
a few Hawaiian words
to combine with English.
This is what many Hawaiians do—
mix languages.

Wiki (wee′ kee) means "hurry."
Can't you hear yourself
telling your mother in the morning
when she's cooking breakfast,
"*Wiki, wiki*"?
Mele (may′ lay) is "song."

"Sing along, gang! Here's
a great *mele!*"
Huhu (hoo′ hoo) is "angry."
"Don't stop me! I'm *huhu!*"
Hapa (hah′ pah) means "half."
"It's *hapa* past eight!"
You already know, probably,
that *aloha* (ah loh′ hah)
means "welcome."
"*Aloha, malihinie.*"
(a-loh-hah mah-lee-hee-nee.)
"Welcome, stranger."
Here are more Hawaiian words
to play with:
luau (loo′ ow) feast,
opu (oh′ poo) stomach
keiki (kay′ kee) child
kaukau (kow′ kow) food,
popoke (poh poh′ kee) cat
pupuli (poo poo′ lee) crazy.

Here are a few English names translated into Hawaiian:

Cynthia	Kinikia	(kee nee kee' ah)
Jane	Kini	(kee' nee)
Judith	Iukiki	(ee oo kee' kee)
Margaret	Makaleka	(man kah lay' kah)
Mary	Malia	(mah lee' ah)
Susan	Suse	(soo' say)
Arthur	Aka	(ah' kah)
David	Kawika	(kah wee' kah)
Edward	Eluwene	(ay loo way' nay)
Frank	Palakiki	(pah lah kee' kee)
Kenneth	Keneke	(kay nay' kay)
Walter	Wala	(wah' lah)

Perhaps you have wondered
why Hawaiian words
are written with English letters.
There is a logical reason.
The Hawaiians had no
    written language
at the time
the first English-speaking
    missionaries
came to the Islands.
As the missionaries began
writing down some
of the Hawaiian words,
they naturally spelled them
with English letters.
If it had been
Japanese missionaries
who had written down
the Hawaiian language,
the language today
very likely would be written
in Japanese characters.
And now for one more word:
humuhumuhunukunukuapuaa.
It's almost as good as
supercalifragilisticexpialidocious.
It's pronounced
(we'll take it in syllables)
hoo-moo-hoo-moo-hoo-noo-koo-noo-koo-
ah-poo-ah-ah.
It's a big name for a little fish
found in the waters around Hawaii.

King of Beasts

The lion is king of the jungle. He fears no other animal on earth, except man. All other animals fear him, including man. Perhaps it would be more correct to say that all other animals fear *her*, because it is the female lion that most often does the hunting and killing for the pride.

An editorial feature
with paintings by Bernard Martin

A pride
is a group
of lions that live
together like a big
family. Most kinds
of cats—the lion belongs
to the cat family—live alone
or in pairs, but lions live in groups
because the group provides them with the sociability[1]
and affection they seem to need. Besides, group membership
is a form of "life insurance" for lions.
When one of the pride becomes sick or wounded, or too old
to hunt, he can depend upon the other lions in the group
to supply him with food.

The pride always includes a dominant[2] male, a few young males,
a large number of females, and many cubs.
The total number of lions in a pride usually is from ten to forty.

[1]The root of this word is *social*.
[2]ruling

However,
all the
members of the pride
seldom gather at one time.
Some of the males often wander away
on mysterious missions for weeks at a time,
and the females leave the pride periodically[3]
to give birth to cubs. A mother lion hides
in a thicket or den to give birth to a litter
of one to four cubs. She keeps the cubs hidden
and nourished for five or six weeks.
Then she brings them back to the pride
and introduces her offspring to the other lions.

When any lion returns to the pride,
even after a short absence, he or she is greeted
by the other lions with genuine affection.

[3]at regular intervals or
periods of time

The others greet the lion
by licking his face
and nestling[4] against his body.

Cubs, once introduced
to the pride,
quickly realize the joys
of being members
of such a large family.
They romp and wrestle
with other cubs of the pride,
play follow-the-leader,
and ambush each other
in mock battle.
The adult lions often join
in the cub games,
but if a cub plays too rough,
or makes a nuisance of himself,
he is apt to be cuffed
on the head by his superiors.[5]

Then, to reassure the cub
that he is still loved,
the adult who punished him
will lovingly lick him
with a long, raspy tongue
to help him get over his hurts
and his bruised feelings.

The full-grown male lions
of a pride
are not hunters.
The female lions are the ones
that supply the pride with food.
Sometimes the males may help
ambush the game,[6]
but more often
they take their rest
under shady trees
and watch while
the lionesses stalk
and kill the game
that will become a feast
for the entire pride.

[4]to cuddle, to press or lie close
[5]those older and more experienced than he

[6]a wild animal hunted for food

The lionesses work as a team
during their daily hunts.
When game is spotted,
one or more females
will approach the prey
as close as possible,
keeping downwind
to avoid being smelled
and flattening out in tall grass
to avoid being seen.
Meanwhile, other lionesses
make a wide circle
around the game.
When they are in good position,
they cough, growl
or roar to alarm
their prey.

This causes the hunted animal
to panic because
there is nothing in the jungle
he fears more than a lion.
Generally, he runs blindly
toward the other lionesses
who are waiting in ambush
to spring upon him.
An experienced lioness
is a sudden and certain killer.
Almost faster
than the eye can follow,
she can leap
upon an impala
or zebra,

break its neck and slit its throat.
Even a large animal,
such as a water buffalo,
is not safe
from the teeth and claws
of a hungry lioness.
A duel between a lioness
and a large buffalo bull

and uproot bushes
and flatten
small trees
before one or the other
is finally killed.
If hungry enough,
a lioness will attack
a full-grown cow elephant,
a rhino or a hippo.
Usually, the lioness
confines her hunt to zebras,
wildebeests, gazelles, impalas,
baboons and wart hogs.

is a
horrifying drama,
as the two fighters
battle up and down
and around and around.
They plow up the earth
over a wide area

Once the game is killed,
the dominant male lion approaches
and cuffs the lioness hunters aside.
The carcass belongs to all the members of the pride,
but all stand back and wait
while the ruler of the pride eats his fill.
Afterwards, the other members of the pride,
young and old, tear into what is left
of the carcass for a noisy meal—
crunching bones, ripping flesh
and growling with pleasure.

People are both frightened and fascinated
by the power, speed, beauty and sound of a lion.
Without weapons, a man is no match for a lion.
When Stone Age man first invented
the spear and the bow-and-arrow,
he became master of the beasts in the jungle.
He even challenged the lion, king of them all.
Killing a lion with a crude weapon was an act
of great courage and skill.
Often it was the lion hunter who lost the battle.
The roar of an angry lion is a terrifying sound.
It causes every hunter to quake
and some to lose their courage.
African natives in the lion country
say the lion's roar means,
"Hii nchi ya nani? Yangu! Yangu!
Whose land is this? Mine! Mine!"

But the fact is,
lions are losing the land in which they roam.
As population has increased, people have claimed
more and more of the lion country for farms and homes.
As the lions lose their hunting grounds,
they die out for lack of food.
Moreover, man[7] has continued
to hunt and kill lions
for sport.
Consequently,
lions have become
fewer and fewer
each year.
At the time
of Christ,
lions ranged widely
over Southern Europe,
the Middle East,
Africa and India.
Today,
lions are found
only in two small areas in Africa and India.
The time may come when lions will be extinct,
just as dinosaurs are now extinct.
The lion still is king of the beasts,
but man, with modern weapons, can force the lion
to give way anytime he wishes.
However, if the lion is to be saved,
only man can do it.

[7]*Man,* in this sentence, means
"the human race."

The Automobile Industry
A Look at the Statistics[1]

It seems to many people
that the automobile
is the pulse of American life.
Today, Americans own
about 86 million automobiles.
Eighty-two per cent
of the Americans
who take transportation to work
go in an automobile.
Ninety-four million Americans
have passed tests
to get driver's licenses.

More than 12 million Americans
work in the auto industry
or in businesses
that are closely connected
to the manufacturing of cars.
This means that 1
out of every 7 people who work
are helping to produce
and service cars.
This also means
that 1 out of 6
of the 800,000 businesses
in this country
produce services and materials
for cars.

The auto industry buys
22 per cent of all steel
produced in the United States.
It buys 60 per cent of the rubber,
90 per cent of the gasoline
and lead,
57 per cent of the malleable[2] iron
35 per cent of the zinc,
75 per cent of the plate glass.

In one year
the auto industry uses
enough plastic vinyl
to cover 12 million
living room sofas,
which would be 1 sofa
for every 5 households
in the United States.
The modern automobile
has 7 miles of wiring in it.
More than half of the radios
in this country
are "on the road."

Automobiles in the future
may run on electricity
rather than gasoline,
and there may even be
electronically-controlled highways
to guide driverless cars
to their destinations.

[1]facts expressed in numbers

[2]iron that can be molded

Buick

1915

52 consecutive years

# of aut motive design

A picture story of progress

Oldsmobile

1916

Oakland

1917

Ford Model "T"

1918

Franklin

1919

Chevrolet

1920

Case

1921

Mercer

1922

Stearns

1923

Chandler

1924

Locomobile

1925

Kissel

1926

Jordan

1927

Ford Model "A"

1928

Plymouth

1929

Cord

1930

Durant
1931

Essex
1932

Dodge
1933

Chrysler Airflow
1934

Cadillac
1935

Terraplane
1936

LaSalle
1937

Ford
1938

Packard
1939

Mercury
1940

Plymouth
1941

Lincoln
1942

Military Amphibian
1943

Willys Jeep
1944

Staff Car (Ford)
1945

DeSoto
1946

Kaiser
1947

Dodge
1948

Ford
1949

Pontiac
1950

Nash Rambler
1951

Plymouth
1952

Mercury
1953

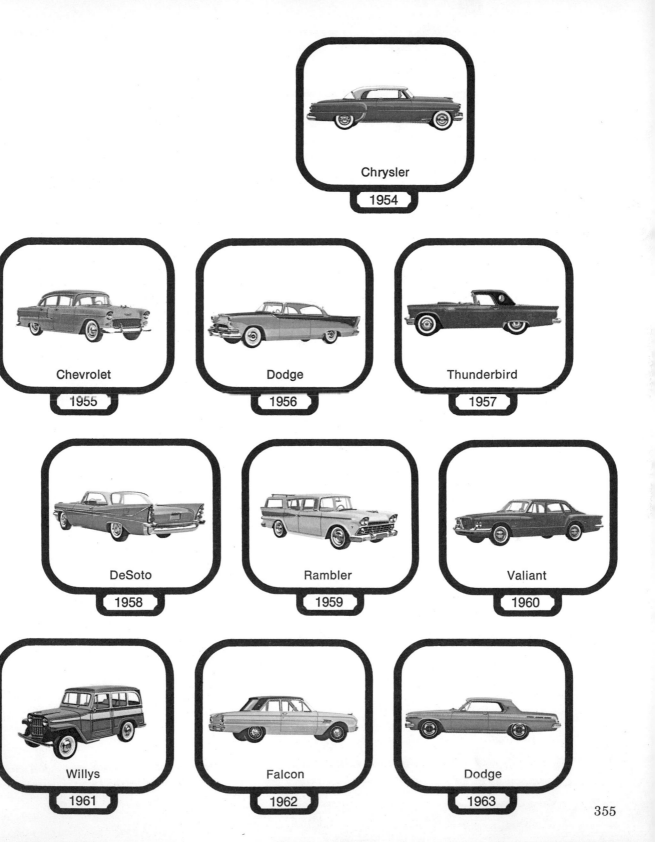

Chrysler
1954

Chevrolet
1955

Dodge
1956

Thunderbird
1957

DeSoto
1958

Rambler
1959

Valiant
1960

Willys
1961

Falcon
1962

Dodge
1963

Chevrolet 1964

Marlin 1965

Mustang 1966

Drawings by Ted Lodigensky

An essay by Bill Martin, Jr.

GOING BEYOND READING

Sometimes your reading may leave you with more questions
than answers. This may happen
           when you think
    that some important inventions have been left out
    of the time line on page 358,
        or when you are reading
    "The Day the Numbers Disappeared," and you get an idea
    that you want to know more about sundials.

There are some things you can do
to simplify your search for information when you need it.
You can seek help from your librarian or teacher
or parents or local businessmen or school friends
or from books in your home or school or favorite bookstore.

An interesting class project sometimes develops
when many members of a class feel
that they need more information on the same subject,
and they group together in their search.

But in whatever directions your questions lead you,
they are part of the rewards of living in a world
where research can help satisfy your curiosity.

Time Line of Inventions

Man is the only creature on earth
that has the ability to invent things.
What he has invented
forms the basis of his civilization.
Here is a *Time Line* of the important inventions,
beginning long before
the calendar itself
was invented
and the dates
of various
inventions
were
recorded.

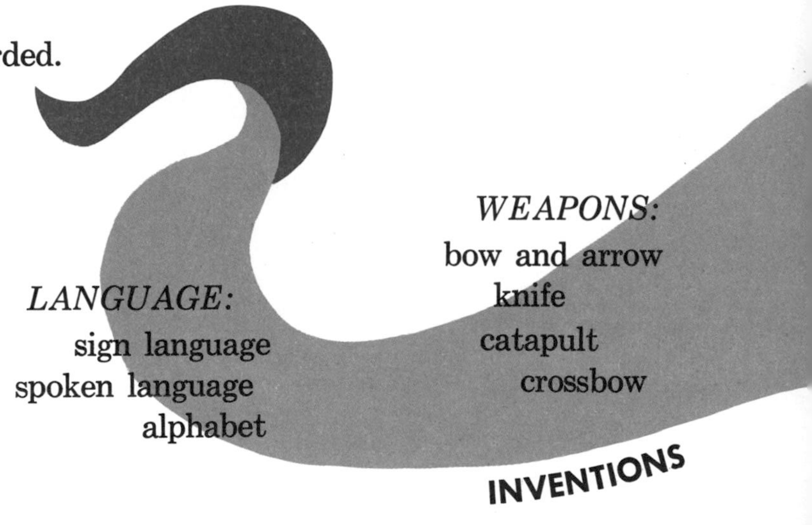

WEAPONS:
bow and arrow
knife
catapult
crossbow

LANGUAGE:
sign language
spoken language
alphabet

INVENTIONS

AGRICULTURE:

seed planting
irrigation methods
animal harness
wooden plow
grape and olive press
hoe and rake

TOOLS:

bone sewing needles
drill (bowstring spun on pointed stick)
screw
axe
saw
carpenter's level
lever
potter's wheel
gears

FIRE:

use of fire for heating and cooking
smelting of metal for tools and weapons
brick making

MEDICINE:

medicine made from plants and minerals

BEFORE TIME WAS RECORDED ON CALENDAR

TRANSPORTATION:
wheel
carts and wagons
raft
hollowed log
canoe
sail-powered boat

MEASUREMENTS:
sundial
abacus
water clock
calendar
mathematics

CLOTH:
rope making
cotton spinning
weaving
hand loom
silk making

COMMUNITY LIVING:
water-supply system
sewage system
mobile housing
permanent housing
systems of government and laws

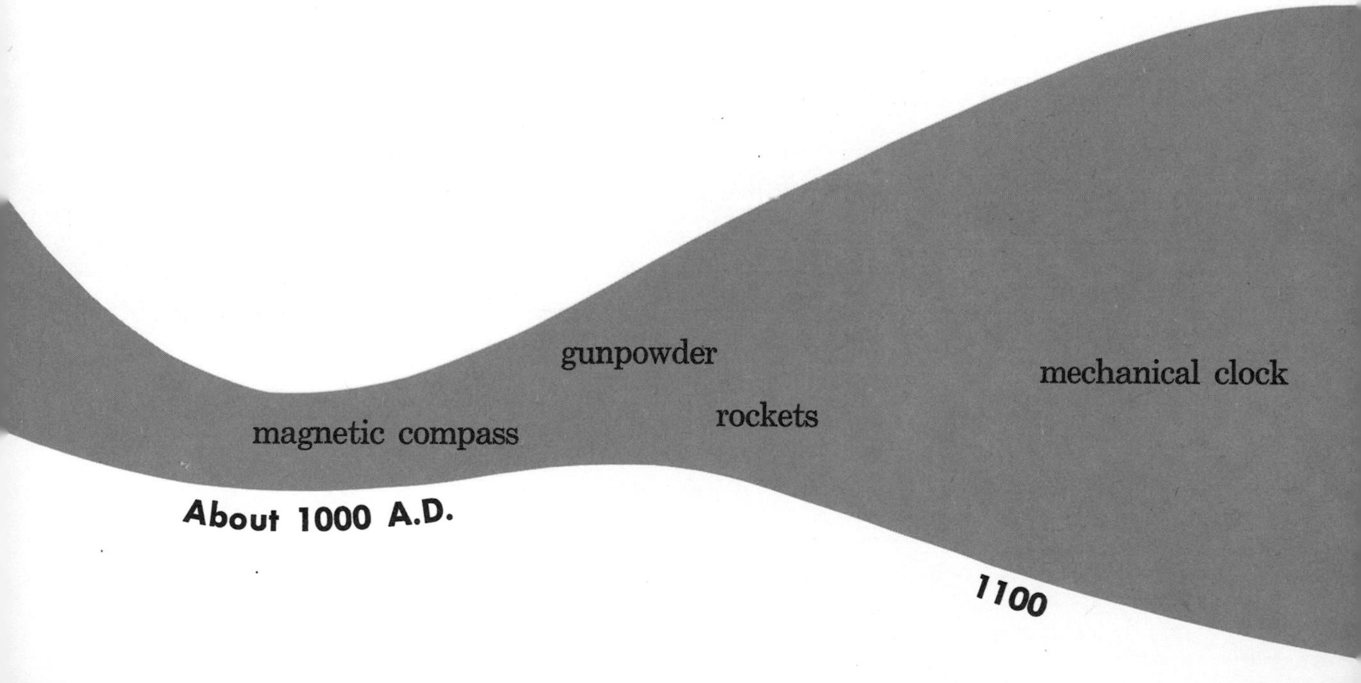

gunpowder

magnetic compass

rockets

mechanical clock

About 1000 A.D.

1100

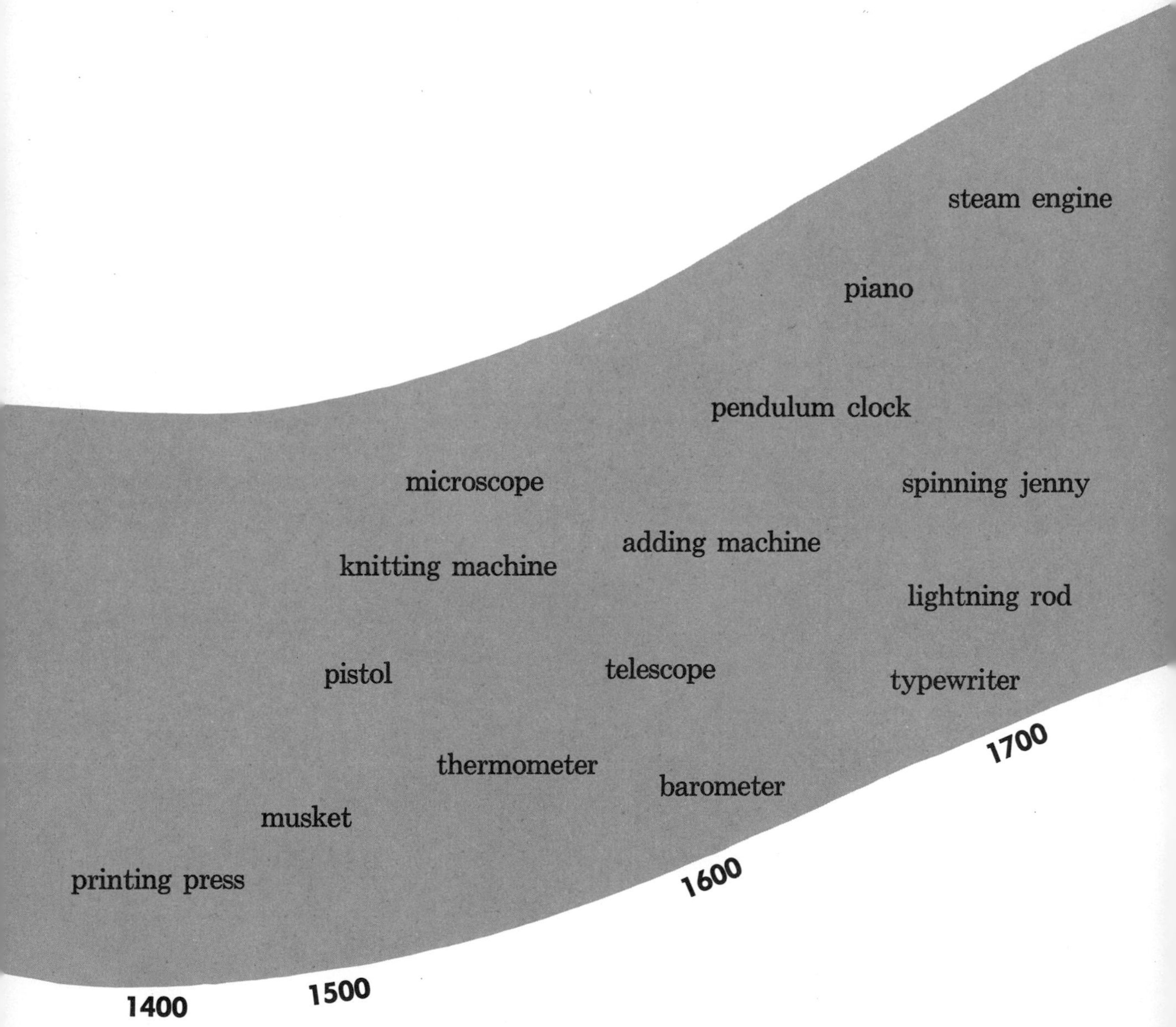
steam engine
piano
pendulum clock
microscope
spinning jenny
adding machine
knitting machine
lightning rod
pistol
telescope
typewriter
1700
thermometer
barometer
musket
1600
printing press
1400
1500

braille printing

food canning

photography

bifocals

mass production assembly line

forerunner of the solar furnace

chloroform as anesthesia

vaccination

magnetic electric generator

power loom

Portland cement

gas light

iron plow

electric telegraph

electric motor

threshing machine

reaper

revolver

steamboat

stethoscope

stecl plow

1775

1800

ether as anesthesia

dynamite

hypodermic needle

telephone

modern bicycle

phonograph

vulcanized rubber

steam turbine

internal combustion engine

refrigerator

color photography

Bunsen burner

antiseptic surgery

sewing machine

steam-powered passenger elevator

Bessemer steel process

machine gun

electric generator

1850

solar steam boiler

1860

electric light

1870

electric automobile

1880

atomic generator

nylon

radar   transistor

solar generator

television   atomic bomb

talking motion pictures

man-made satellite

modern submarine   jet propulsion engine

manned spaceships

wireless telegraph   iron lung

hydrogen bomb

airplane   liquid-fueled rocket

solar battery

process for freezing foods

X-ray photography

artificial heart

tractor   cyclotron   atomic reactor

radio tube   electric automobile

remote radio control

silent motion pictures

plastics

1890   1900   1910   1920   1930   1940   1950   PRESENT   FUTURE

Vacation Time

A picture for pondering by Joe Veno

The children in this story (taken from Leonard Simon's intriguing book The Day the Numbers Disappeared) *create a mystery that will take some doing to solve. What kind of problem-solver are you? Time will tell.*

THE DAY NUMBERS DISAPPEAR

The whole class loved Mr. Dibbs.
They could hardly wait to get to school in the morning, it was such fun having him for a teacher. And when they got home, they were popping with things they had learned from Mr. Dibbs.

Mr. Dibbs said he learned things from them, too. "You'd be surprised," he said "how many things I learn from this class."

A story by Leonard Simon and Jeanne Bendick,
picture by Frank Aloise

Mr. Dibbs and the class were so pleased with each other that THE FIGHT came as a surprise to everybody. The fight was over arithmetic. It started when Mr. Dibbs was writing the arithmetic lesson on the board. He distinctly heard three groans and four sighs. He put down the chalk and turned around.

"And what is the matter with arithmetic?" he asked.

Steve sighed. "I guess I just don't like arithmetic, Mr. Dibbs. In fact, I don't like numbers. I  wish we didn't have any."

"They're dull," said Cathy.

"Who needs them?" David asked.

Mr. Dibbs looked thoughtfully around the class. "Well," he said. "Does everybody feel that way?"

"You *bet!*" shouted four more pupils at the same time.

Mr. Dibbs sat on a corner of his desk and whistled quietly to himself for a minute. "It's hard for me to understand," he said, "because I *love* numbers. I like number marks and the things you can do with them. I like arithmetic. But of course, everyone to his own taste, as the old lady said, kissing the cow."

"Do you really think," Mr. Dibbs asked, "that things would be easier without numbers and the marks for them?"

Everybody nodded.

"Are you prepared to defend your belief in a fair fight?" Mr. Dibbs asked solemnly. "Are you prepared to prove to me that arithmetic is only a nuisance? Because if you are, we'll start tomorrow. No numbers and no arithmetic."

The class cheered.

"Just a minute," Mr. Dibbs interrupted. "If you lose the fight, you have to pay the penalty."

"Who cares?" Steve grinned. "No numbers and no arithmetic tomorrow? What a break!"

When the class came in the next morning, Mr. Dibbs looked like a boy on his way to the circus.

"Larry, you take the lunch orders," he said.

Larry stood up. "Everyone who wants lunch today, raise your hand . . ."

Mr. Dibbs interrupted. "What are you doing?"

"Why, I'm counting the number . . ." Larry said.

"Counting?" said Mr. Dibbs. "What's that? There's no such thing as counting. You'll just have to write down all the names, and when you go to the cafeteria, you'll have to match a lunch to each name. That's what people did before they had numbers."

"That will take *forever*," Larry wailed.

"Oh, well," said Mr. Dibbs calmly. "It doesn't matter, because time doesn't mean anything to you now."

"All right," Larry sighed. "Those who want lunch, put the money on your desk."

"How are you going to count it or figure out change without using numbers?" Mr. Dibbs asked.

"Maybe we could charge it," Hallie said hopefully.

"It must be time for the science television lesson. Danny, will you turn on the set, please?" said Mr. Dibbs.

The class looked at the clock, but it was blank. Somebody had covered the face, and all the numbers were gone.

Do you think you could figure out

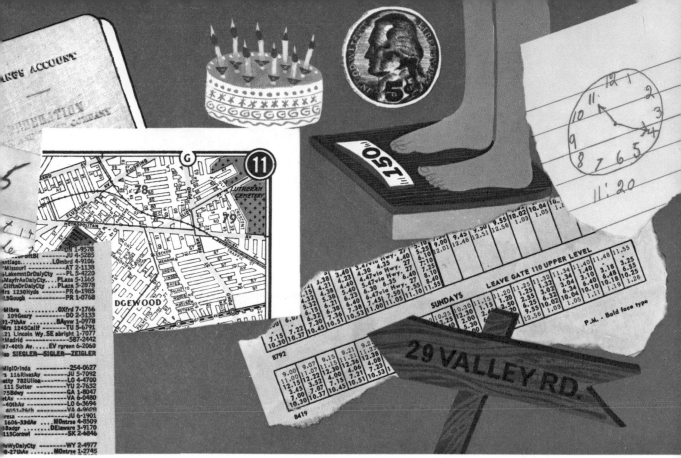

Montage by Robert and Jack Strimban

"What time is it?" Willa asked. "We've probably missed half of the program already."

Yes they missed part of the science lesson.

After it was over, the class had to finish the invitations they were writing to their parents to visit school. Mr. Dibbs walked around the class, watching, as they started to address the envelopes.

"What are you doing there, friend Ralph?" he asked suddenly.

"I'm writing my home address on the envelope."

Mr. Dibbs shook his head. "But don't you remember, you can't use any number marks today."

Ralph looked confused. "But how can you address an envelope without them?"

"Don't ask *me!*" said Mr. Dibbs. "What you can figure out."

how to live for a day without using numbers and number marks? Try it.

October

O hushed October
morning mild,
Thy leaves have ripened
to the fall;
Tomorrow's wind,
if it be wild,
Should waste them all.
The crows
above the forest call;
Tomorrow they may form
and go.
O hushed October
morning mild,
Begin the hours
of this day slow.

An excerpt from the poem by Robert Frost,
painting by Stanley Maltzman

Antelope

Elk

Animals that helped

Beaver

Mule Deer

The first trailblazers
of the American West
were wild animals.
For thousands of years
before the coming
of trappers and settlers,
wild animals roamed the land
west of the Mississippi River.
Enormous herds of buffalo
and elk and deer and antelope
surged across the prairies
and through the mountain passes
in their never-ending search
for new grazing grounds.
By instinct,
by trial
and error,
they found
and followed the easiest
and most natural pathways
across the continent.
And it was these very trails
that made it possible
for the American pioneers
to settle the lands
west of the Mississippi.
The pioneers would not have known
the best ways to cross
the mountains and rivers
and grudging slopes
if they had not followed
the animal trails.

Buffalo

win the West

An essay by Bernard Martin,
pictures by Jim Walker

This picture of an old-time trapper was painted by a distinguished contemporary artist, John Clymer. In what ways is this a picture of trapping? How does the picture tell what Mr. Clymer wanted it to tell?

Other wild animals
that were instrumental
in the settlement of the West
were those that tempted trappers
into the unsettled territory
with their valuable furs.
One such animal was the beaver.
Prior to 1800,
fifty million beaver
were believed to have inhabited
the region west
of the Mississippi.
The beaver's coat
of rich, lustrous, brown fur
was worth ten dollars or more
to fur traders
in St. Louis and New York.
The presence
of millions of beaver
in the streams and rivers
of the frontier
represented a great opportunity
for riches
to many buckskin-clad trappers.
It lured[1] them   [1]enticed, beckoned
into every nook and cranny
of the vast wilderness.
   The trappers raced
up the Missouri River
to set beaver traps
on the Platte,
the Snake, the Clearwater
and the Yellowstone rivers.

Here is another picture by John Clymer about trappers in the olden days. The picture communicates much about a trapper's life that the story doesn't. How does this picture tell you what it wants to say?

Others ventured
into the Southwest
along the Colorado River
and its tributaries.
   As the trappers
continually searched
for new and better
trapping territory,
they used the trails
made by the buffalo
and other animals,
and they made maps of the land
to guide others
through the wilderness.
   When settlers began
to flow westward,
many trappers were paid
to guide them
across the hard
and often hostile[2] land.   [2]unfriendly
Basing their routes on the trails
that had been used by animals
for thousands of years,
the trappers laid out
the Santa Fe, the Oregon
and the Mormon trails,
plus dozens of minor[3] routes   [3]less important
leading across the continent
to the Pacific Ocean.

        As the frontier
moved slowly westward
year by year,
animals of all kinds
were killed for food, clothes,
shelter and sport.
By 1890,
the great herds of buffalo
and untold millions
of brown-furred beaver
had almost become extinct.[4]   [4]no longer living
And with the disappearance
of the animals,
the trapper, too, soon vanished
and receded into history.
However, he left a legacy[5]   [5]gift from the past
of trails over which
a stream of settlers
poured across the prairies
and mountains to the Pacific.
Stagecoaches followed
the wagon trains,
and the railroad
followed the stagecoaches,
and all of them followed
the animal trails
of the old West.
Even trains and cars traveling
across the country today
are following those routes
which, not so very long ago,
thundered under the hoofs
of mighty buffalo herds.

The Flower-Fed Buffaloes

The flower-fed buffaloes of the spring
In the days of long ago
Ranged where the locomotives sing
And the prairie flowers lie low;
The tossing, blooming, perfumed grass
Is swept away by wheat,
Wheels and wheels and wheels spin by
In the spring that still is sweet.
But the flower-fed buffaloes of the spring
Left us long ago.
They gore no more, they bellow no more,
They trundle around the hills no more:—
With the Blackfeet lying low,
With the Pawnees lying low.

A poem by Vachel Lindsay,
picture by Chet Reneson

making judgments

As you think back on this book, what five things
did you like best? You can choose anything
between the covers—stories, poems, essays, pictures, words,
titles, sentences, articles, songs, anything.
After your list is made and you study your choices,
what does it tell you about yourself?

> Are these the same kind of choices
> > you would have made a year ago?
>
> Is there anything in your list
> > that you had to learn to like?
>
> Is there anyone else in the class
> > who chose exactly the same things you did?

And now for the most important question of all:

> Do you know why you made the choices you did?

That is a question not easily answered.
You may be asking yourself that question for a lifetime.

An essay by Bill Martin, Jr.

Of this you can be sure, however.

As you live in and out of books,

taking in their messages and wonder,

your choices in art and literature and language and ideas

will be changing constantly.

And if you would like to see your "tracks" in making choices,

you might like to start now, keeping a list of your

> 5 favorite stories
>
> or 5 favorite pictures
>
> or 5 favorite poems
>
> or 5 favorite books
>
> or 5 favorite artists
>
> or 5 favorite sentences
>
> or 5 favorite songs
>
> or 5 favorite words.

Your search for new favorites should be never-ending,

going on and on and on.

Whenever you find a new favorite and add it to your list,

remove one of the old favorites already there.

In other words, when you add one, you take one out.

A project of this kind not only will help you know

what you like, but also will help you know

why you choose what you do.

Illustration by Frank Aloise

Beyond the Mountains

There lies a world beyond the mountains,
There lies a world for me to see.
And I must go beyond the mountains,
And leave the home so dear to me.

My father lived beneath the mountains,
As did his father long ago,
And I was born
      beneath the mountains.
      They are the only home I know.

And so, farewell,
      O friendly mountains.
The time has come for me to roam,
And e'er I go
      beyond the mountains,
I know my heart will long for home.

English lyrics by Marilyn
Keith and Alan Bergman
from the song "Switzerland,"
painting by Lydia Rosier